MASTERING WOODWORKING™

APPLYING FINISHES

MASTERING WOODWORKING™

APPLYING FINISHES

Techniques, Tips, and Problem-Solving Tricks

BOB FLEXNER
Author of the Best-Selling *Understanding Wood Finishing*

Rodale Press, Inc.
Emmaus, Pennsylvania

© 1997 by Rodale Press, Inc.

The author and editors who compiled this book have tried to make all of the contents as accurate and as correct as possible. Plans, illustrations, photographs, and text have all been carefully checked and cross-checked. However, due to the variability of local conditions, construction materials, personal skill, and so on, neither the authors nor Rodale Press assumes any responsibility for any injuries suffered or for damages or other losses incurred that result from the material presented herein. All instructions and plans should be carefully studied and clearly understood before beginning construction.

Printed in the United States of America on acid-free ∞ , recycled ♻ paper

Mastering Woodworking: Applying Finishes Editorial Staff

Editor: Ken Burton
Project Writers: Ken Burton, Tony O'Malley
Book Designer: Jan Melchior
Cover and Interior Illustrator: Glenn Hughes
Interior Photographer: Mitch Mandel
Interior Photo Stylist: Marianne Grape Laubach
Cover Photographer: John Hamel
Technical Artist: Dale Mack
Copy Editors: Elizabeth Leone Barone,
 Barbara McIntosh Webb
Manufacturing Coordinator: Melinda B. Rizzo
Indexer: Nan N. Badgett
Editorial Assistance: Sue Nickol, Jodi Rehl, Lori Schaffer
Project Designers:
 Ken Burton: Display-Top Coffee Table
 Tony O'Malley: Game Box, Kitchen Cart,
 Compact Disc Cabinet
Rodale Design Shop: Fred Matlack

Rodale Home and Garden Books

Vice President and Editorial Director:
 Margaret J. Lydic
Managing Editor, Woodworking and DIY Books:
 Kevin Ireland
Art Director: Paula Jaworski
Studio Manager: Leslie Keefe
Copy Director: Dolores Plikaitis
Production Manager: Helen Clogston
Office Manager: Karen Earl-Braymer

Location for photos on pages 14 and 30 courtesy of Builders Square, Allentown, Pennsylvania

If you have any questions or comments concerning the editorial content of this book, please write to:
 Rodale Press, Inc.
 Book Readers' Service
 33 East Minor Street
 Emmaus, PA 18098

Library of Congress Cataloging-in-Publication Data

Flexner, Bob
 Applying finishes / Bob Flexner
  p. cm. –(Mastering woodworking)
 Includes index.
 ISBN 0–87596–747–7 (hardcover : alk. paper)
 1. Wood finishing. 2. Stains and staining.
 3. Furniture finishing. I. Title II. Series
 TT325.F5297 1996
 684.1'043—dc 20   96–25125

Distributed in the book trade by St. Martin's Press

2 4 6 8 10 9 7 5 3 1 hardcover

APR 18 1997

ABOUT BOB FLEXNER

Bob Flexner has operated a furniture-making and refinishing shop for 20 years. In the late 1980s he became so frustrated with the lack of accurate information about wood finishes that he began studying the chemistry of these products himself.

After absorbing much of the science behind the craft, he started writing about what he had learned, translating much of the jargon into straightforward, easy-to-understand language.

In this book, as well as in his first book, *Understanding Wood Finishing*, Flexner has cut through a lot of the myths and lore surrounding the craft of finishing to make it accessible to everyone.

He also conducts workshops on the subjects of finishing and furniture restoration and contributes to numerous woodworking magazines.

Contents

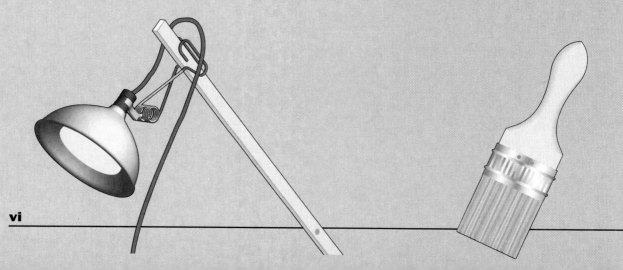

Projects

INTRODUCTION

If you're like most of the woodworkers I've talked to, you don't particularly like finishing. And from what people have told me, it's not that finishing is overly physically demanding or intolerably messy. Woodworking is at least as bad on both counts. The reason that finishing is so disliked is that it seems so unpredictable. Something is always going wrong, and the causes are seldom readily apparent.

The fear of problems in finishing leads most woodworkers to avoid trying anything new, and often leads them to use nothing more demanding than oil or oil/varnish-blend finishes. These finishes, though almost foolproof to apply, offer little possibility for decoration and almost no protection for the wood against wear and moisture-vapor exchange. So how can finishing be made more controllable and thus more fun? I suggest you change your approach.

All too many woodworkers expect finishing to be problem-free. Everything should go exactly right. This attitude is cultivated by manufacturers of finishing products and by publishers, who promote their products and information as producing "professional results" or "perfect finishes"

every time. But no craft can be so trouble-free. You know this about woodworking. No matter how much you practice, you continue to make mistakes. And even if you don't make a mistake, the wood is apt to move when you least want it to. The trick to mastering a craft is knowing how to fix the mistakes.

If you are one of the countless woodworkers who don't like finishing, here are a couple of lessons that may help change your attitude.

First, realize that practice and experimentation are the only ways you're going to build your finishing skills. You practice your woodworking skills, like cutting dovetail joints on scrap wood before you try them on your good walnut, so why not take the same approach with finishing?

Before you commit a stain to your next project (which probably took several weeks to build), open this book and read up on stains and how they work. Then try the stain out on some scraps. Or go a step further and try something new (on those same scraps, of course), like filling the pores or rubbing out the finish to a high gloss. Then at least you'll know

what to expect when you are ready to tackle the real thing.

Second, keep in mind that when you make a serious mistake in woodworking, such as cutting a board too short or cutting dovetails backward, you don't throw up your hands in resignation that you have no talent for the craft. You just start over with new wood and are more careful the second time. You can use the same process in finishing.

Except for blotchy staining, all problems in finishing can be fixed with very little effort—the worst case being that you have to strip off the finish and start over.

Stripping and starting over is not pleasant, but neither is making a new wood part. People commonly strip and refinish old furniture. It may help to remember that all professional finishers and refinishers, who practice the craft every day, still have to strip and start over far more often than they would like. Don't think that there is something wrong with you just because you make mistakes now and then. If you could get it right every time, the craft would lose its challenge.

Bob Flexner

Bob Flexner

TECHNIQUES

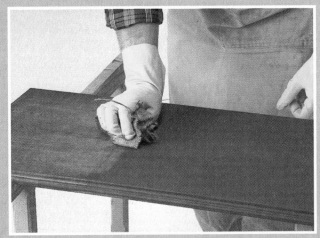

1
WOOD PREPARATION

Key Ingredients

It can't be overemphasized how important wood preparation is for obtaining a nice-looking finish. Stains and finishes highlight flaws rather than disguise them. You can't achieve first-rate results if you don't do a good job preparing the wood first. Sharp tools, clean hands, and good work habits all go a long way toward making this initial preparation a less daunting task.

The goal in wood preparation is to remove all flaws and not replace them with new ones, as shown in the photos. The machine tools you use to cut, smooth, and shape wood all leave marks (called machine marks, mill marks, or milling marks) that show up when you apply a stain or finish. These marks should be hand-planed, scraped, or sanded out.

Excess glue is a problem as well. Glue can keep stain from penetrating and can cause uneven coloring. It may be squeezed from joints or deposited onto the wood by dirty hands. You should remove this glue before applying a stain or finish.

Any gouges and gaps also must be dealt with, either by sanding them out or by filling them in one way or another. The obvious solution—wood putty—may not be the best answer because it rarely takes stain as the wood does, no matter what manufacturers may claim. If you choose to go this route, you should use a colored wood putty, or color the wood

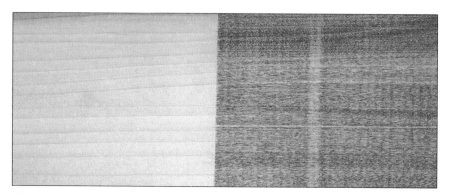

You can't get good results finishing if you don't prepare the wood well. Machine marks that are practically invisible on an unfinished board really stand out under a coat of stain.

Excess glue leaves a telltale mark under stains and finishes. Not only does it look bad, it also detracts from the overall quality of the project.

putty after it has dried to blend in with the surrounding wood.

On top of all this, bear in mind that the sandpaper and tools you use to remove flaws may actually create new flaws. Power sanders in particular remove wood so fast that it's easy to go too far and create divots and

furrows on an otherwise flat surface. Even hand sanding can leave scratches that will jump out at you the moment you apply the first coat of stain. Always sand in the direction of the wood grain, using several grits, increasingly finer, until the scratches that are left are too fine to be seen.

Most woodworkers use wood putty now and then. But special care is required if you don't want the putty to broadcast its presence from beneath a finish since no putty takes a stain just like the surrounding wood.

Sanding is the answer to many wood preparation problems, but it can also cause trouble. Power sanders that get out of hand can leave a less than flat surface; sanding across the grain leaves ugly scratches that are emphasized by stain.

THREE HAND-HELD SANDING MACHINES

While furniture factories can indulge in large, stationary sanding equipment, small shops are generally restricted to hand-held sanders. Orbital sanders are the cheapest and least efficient of the three commonly available tools. They leave swirl patterns in the wood that often don't show up until you apply a stain. Always finish the surface by hand sanding in the direction of the grain, using your final-grit sandpaper. This will remove the orbital scratches.

Belt sanders remove a lot of wood quickly, but they are difficult to control. The slightest rocking of the sander will leave a gouge in the surface that will take a lot of work to sand out. With enough practice, however, it is possible to use a belt sander effectively.

Random-orbit sanders are fast becoming the hand sander of choice for most woodworkers. These use a round sanding disc and move it in a random, circular pattern that leaves a very light scratch pattern. These scratches, however, often show when you apply a stain. It is good practice to finish off by hand sanding with the grain, using your final-grit sandpaper.

Power sanding for most woodworkers means using one of three tools: the orbital sander (left), the belt sander (middle), or the random-orbit sander (right). While these can save time, it is generally best to follow up with a little hand sanding to get the best results.

Sanding Wood

The reason you sand wood is to remove machine marks. All machine tools leave cuts or impressions in wood that are highlighted by finishes—especially stains. Before machine tools were developed in the mid-nineteenth century, no sanding was needed; indeed, there was no sandpaper. Wood was smoothed with hand planes and scrapers.

You can still use hand planes and scrapers to smooth wood without using a single sheet of sandpaper. Work straight from the saw, or begin the smoothing with a jointer and planer and then finish off with a hand plane or scraper. You can also use molding planes and scratch stocks to shape wood, rather than routers and shapers.

Few woodworkers choose this route, because machine tools are much faster and easier to learn to use than hand tools. The price, however, is that you have to sand out the machine marks. This is an important psychological point. Sanding seems less burdensome when you remind yourself that you don't have to do it.

How to Sand

The trick to efficient sanding is beginning with a grit coarse enough to cut through the flaws you want to remove with the least amount of effort, without creating larger scratches than necessary. This holds true whether you are sanding by hand or machine. In practice, the best grit to begin with is usually 80 or 100. If the problems are so severe that 80-grit doesn't remove them quickly, drop back to a grit that does.

On the other hand, if the problems can be removed with a finer-grit sandpaper, such as 120 or 150, you are wasting time and energy if you begin sanding with coarser sandpaper. (Many people begin sanding stripped wood with 100-grit sandpaper, when no more than a light pass with 180- or 220-grit would be necessary to ensure that all the finish has been removed. The wood was sanded originally, after all.)

Once the flaws are gone, sand out scratches left by the coarse-grit sandpaper using increasingly finer sandpapers until you reach a grit that produces the size scratches you want. The scratch sizes make a difference in color intensity when using a pigment stain, as shown in the photo. The best grit to end with is usually 180 or 220. I usually stop at 180-grit. The goal is to produce a surface that doesn't show machine marks or sanding scratches after you apply a stain or finish. If the scratch pattern can be made even, you may achieve satisfactory results sanding to only 120- or 150-grit. Stationary sanding machines do this best.

If you could sand just the right amount with each sandpaper grit, it would be most efficient to go through each consecutive grit—80, 100, 120, 150, 180. But most of us sand more than necessary with each grit, so we find that we actually spend less

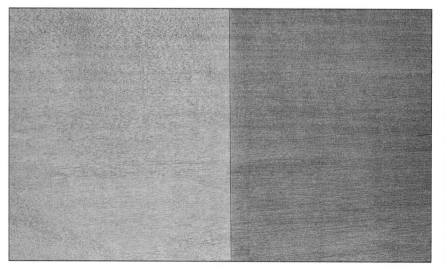

The finer the grit you sand to, the less a pigment stain colors the wood. This is because there is less room in each sanding scratch for pigment to lodge. The lighter side of this board was sanded to 280, the darker side only to 100.

FACT OR FICTION

THE FINER THE GRIT, THE BETTER?

You often hear that sanding wood to 400 grit or higher produces better results. It does make the wood look and feel better in its raw state. But fine sanding doesn't add anything to the appearance or feel once you have applied a film finish, such as polyurethane, lacquer, or water-based finish, and it takes away from the effectiveness of pigment stains because less pigment lodges in fine scratches. Fine sanding does make a difference when you are applying a non-building finish like oil or wax, but you can achieve the same smooth appearance and feel with much less work by sanding the finish with fine-grit sandpaper (400-grit or 600-grit) between coats.

effort if we skip grits. This is especially the case when using machine-sanding tools.

But sanding is very personal. We apply different pressures, use sandpapers to different degrees of wear, and sand for varying lengths of time. The only way to know for sure that you have sanded enough is to apply a stain and see if any machine marks or sanding scratches show. It is therefore wise to practice on some scrap wood until you get a feel for what works best for you.

RAISING DENTS

It happens to everyone—a dropped tool or an errant hammer blow and suddenly you have a big dent right where you don't want one. Before you reach for the sander or scraper, you should know that not all dents and dings are permanent. With a little luck, you may be able to steam the dent out, as shown in the photos to the right. Then, with a little light sanding, no one will ever know what happened.

The dents that respond best to steaming are those where the wood fibers are only compressed, not broken. Compressed fibers will usually swell right back to their original shape.

Dents that involve broken fibers can be steamed, but you will always be able to see a scar where the dent was. Depending on the severity of the dent, some additional filler may be necessary.

If you must fill a partially steamed dent, you can try to match the color of the filler to the surrounding wood—a time consuming ordeal at best. A better solution might be to go with a contrasting filler. There are usually enough variations in the color of a piece of wood that a small contrasting patch will simply look like a natural defect.

A pressure mark such as this is a good candidate for steaming. The wood fibers are compressed but not broken.

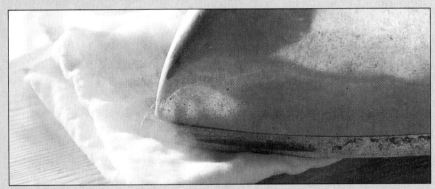

Apply a wet rag to the surface and heat it with an iron. The resulting steam will expand the dented wood fibers.

In most cases, the dent will practically disappear. Steaming will probably raise the grain as well, so some touch-up sanding may be in order.

SHOP SOLUTIONS: Two Sanding Aids

Here are two handy devices I've made to make sanding a little less tedious. The first is a light that helps me see exactly what I'm doing.

To get an idea whether any coarser-grit scratches remain from a previous sanding, look at the sanded surface lengthwise in a raking light occasionally as you move through the grits. A raking light creates a very low-level reflection across the surface, as shown in the photo below.

While you could use a hand-held light for this, I made up a stand to hold a clamp-on unit, as shown in *A Sanding Light.* You can clamp the light anywhere along the upright, and you can tilt the upright to hold the light just where you want it.

After making the stand, I have found other uses for it in the shop. I often use it to throw light right on the band saw and other tools so I can really see what I'm doing.

The second device is a cork-faced sanding block. If you are

sanding a flat surface like a table-top, and you want to keep it flat, you should always back your sandpaper with a flat cork, felt, or rubber block. The block should be firm, yet soft enough to absorb any coarser-grit dirt that

Shine a light across your boards at a low angle to help you spot sanding scratches that need to be removed with a finer-grit sandpaper.

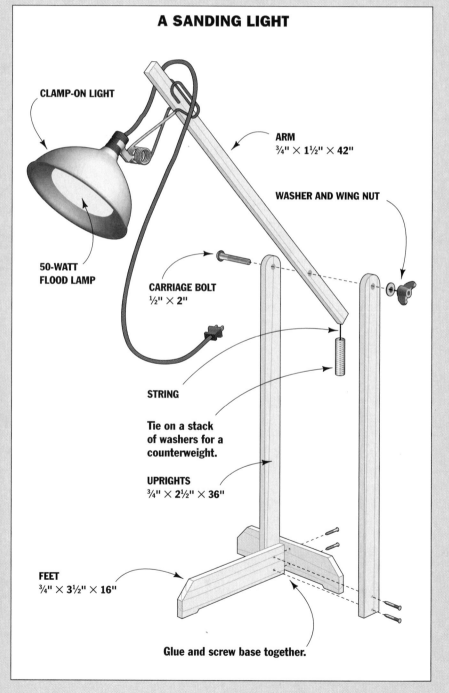

A SANDING LIGHT

CLAMP-ON LIGHT

ARM
3/4" × 1 1/2" × 42"

WASHER AND WING NUT

50-WATT FLOOD LAMP

CARRIAGE BOLT
1/2" × 2"

STRING

Tie on a stack of washers for a counterweight.

UPRIGHTS
3/4" × 2 1/2" × 36"

FEET
3/4" × 3 1/2" × 16"

Glue and screw base together.

may get trapped between it and the sandpaper or between the sandpaper and the wood. (I find the commercially available rubber sanding blocks to be too hard.)

You can make a block to fit your hand by gluing some 1/8-inch gasket cork, available at auto parts stores, to a wood block that is chamfered on the top side, as shown in *A Sanding Block*. Use softwood to keep the weight down.

The measurements shown fit my hand well and use a piece of sandpaper very efficiently. I cut or tear the standard 8 × 11-inch sandpaper sheet in thirds across the width, fold each third in half crosswise, as shown in *Folding Sandpaper*, and sand with both

sides; then I unfold the sandpaper, wrap it around the block, and sand with the unused middle part. This way, I can make use of almost 100 percent of each sheet of sandpaper.

Note that folding the sandpaper this way never results in grit-to-grit contact. This keeps the sandpaper from wearing itself out.

A SANDING BLOCK

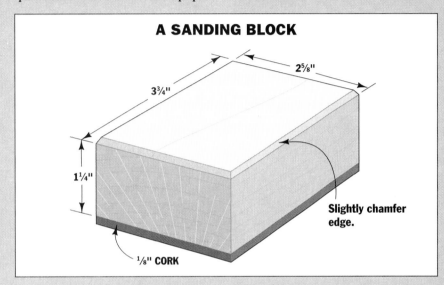

2⅝"

3¾"

1¼"

Slightly chamfer edge.

⅛" CORK

FOLDING SANDPAPER

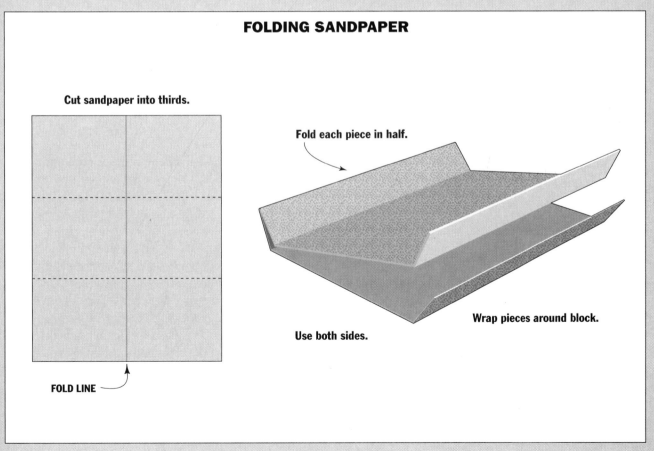

Cut sandpaper into thirds.

Fold each piece in half.

Wrap pieces around block.

Use both sides.

FOLD LINE

Filling In Gouges and Gaps

You probably try to make your woodworking perfect, avoiding gaps in the joints, as well as dings and gouges in the surfaces. Despite your best efforts, however, mistakes do occur and you have to fix them. It is always better to patch problems with real wood (solid or veneer) than with wood putty. Real wood takes stain like the surrounding wood, as long as you use the same kind of wood and make sure that the grain direction is the same.

The problem is that it requires more work to make a wood patch than to simply stuff in some wood putty. On the other hand, wood putty doesn't take stain as wood does.

What Is Wood Putty?

Most commercial wood putties are made with wood flour (very fine sawdust) and some type of finish that cures and binds the wood flour particles to each other and to the wood.

Pack the putty into the depression with a putty knife.

Homemade wood putties are typically mixtures of sawdust and glue, usually white glue or epoxy. Since neither finish nor glue can absorb common stain, it's simply not possible to make a wood putty that will stain as naturally as wood.

There are three common types of commercial wood putties: nitrocellulose lacquer-based, waterborne acrylic finish-based, and gypsum-(plaster of paris) based. You can tell which kind you have from the instructions on the container. Nitrocellulose-based wood putties state that they can be thinned and cleaned up with acetone or lacquer thinner. Waterborne acrylic-based wood putties can be cleaned up with water. Gypsum-based putties come in powder form that you are instructed to mix with water.

Applying Wood Putty

Each of these wood putties is applied in a similar manner. Take a little of the putty out of the container or tube with a putty knife (or screwdriver if the hole to be filled is small). Push the putty down in the hole or gouge, and if the depression is not very deep, smooth off the top by pulling the putty knife across the surface towards you, as shown in the photos. You want the putty to form a very slight mound so that it won't leave a depression when it shrinks as it dries. If the depression is deep, it's best to apply several coats to build the putty level with the surface. Don't manipulate the putty any more than necessary since it becomes increasingly unworkable the longer it's exposed to the air.

Once the putty is thoroughly cured, sand it level with the surrounding wood. If you're working on a flat surface, back the sandpaper with a flat block.

Smooth the surface with the knife. You want to leave the putty slightly mounded to allow for shrinkage.

Matching Color

You can use universal tinting colors, available at most paint or art-supply stores, to color any type of putty, commercial or homemade. The color you want to match is that of the wood after it is stained and finished. It may take some experimentation on scrap wood to arrive at this color. The trick is to judge the color while the putty is still damp. At that stage you'll get a fairly good idea of how the putty will look under a finish. The color of the stain or putty when dry will not be accurate.

Coloring the putty before applying it is an easy way to approximate wood, but you can get better results by coloring the patch after it is dry and has been sanded smooth, as shown in the photo on the opposite page. Coloring the putty after application allows you to imitate the colors in the surrounding wood more exactly. Essentially, you are painting the putty to look like wood.

For the coloring medium, you can use glaze or thinned varnish with some japan or oil color added. Or you can use shellac or padding lacquer and add special powdered pigment colors or universal colors. The advantage of glaze and thinned varnish is that if you don't like the result, you can remove the finish by wiping with paint thinner. The dis-

Wood isn't any single color, so it is no wonder monochromatic putty patches look bad. You'll have better luck with putty if you take the time to color it to match the various colors surrounding it.

advantage is that this alternative takes overnight to cure. The advantage of shellac and padding lacquer is speed (the finish dries fast). But mistakes aren't easily reversible because shellac and padding lacquer bite into most finishes. Sometimes you can remove the coloring by wiping over lightly with alcohol. It's normally safest, however, to abrade off the coloring using steel wool.

STEP 1 To color a patch, apply your first coat of finish (the sealer coat) to the entire surface, putty and all, in order to see the correct colors you want to imitate. This also creates a nonporous surface for painting.

STEP 2 Once this sealer coat is dry, paint in the grain and figure using an artist's brush. You may also want to scratch pores into the patch with the point of a knife to imitate deep-porous woods such as oak, mahogany, or walnut.

STEP 3 Once you have a close approximation of the grain, let the patch dry and protect it with a thin coat of finish.

STEP 4 Then apply the background color (the lightest color visible in the surrounding wood). If you

paint the background first, you'll probably get the patch too dark when you paint the grain.

As an alternative, you can use a hybrid of the two techniques. Use a putty that matches the lighter color of wood. Then add the darker grain and figure lines.

Drawing in grain and figure can be done only on film finishes, such as shellac, lacquer, varnish, polyurethane, and water-based finishes. Oil and oil/varnish-blend finishes are too thin to color between coats.

THREE REASONS WOOD-PUTTY PATCHES DON'T LOOK LIKE WOOD

1 Any given section of wood has many colors in various patterns. To match perfectly, the putty would have to mimic both the colors and the patterns. But wood putty isn't made to show different colors—it is a uniform substance that stains uniformly. Even if someone were able to make a wood putty that stained like one of the colors in a piece of wood, the patch

still wouldn't look like the surrounding wood because it would still be a single, uniform color.

2 Wood has pores and wood putty doesn't. Even if wood putty could be made to cure with pore-like cavities, what size should they be? Large and irregular like oak? Medium-sized and regular like mahogany? Or very small like maple?

3 How do you get a substance that turns from a liquid or paste to a fairly nonporous solid to take stain at all? Only solids that are porous can take stain. And even if you could make filler porous, once again you would be faced with the problem of which porosity to imitate. The relatively open porosity of poplar? Or the tight porosity of maple?

Avoiding Glue Seepage

O ne of the biggest problems you'll face in preparing wood for a stain or finish is glue getting on the wood's surface. It happens when glue squeezes out of a joint, or when you touch the wood with glue on your fingertips.

Ideally, you should control the amount of glue you put into a joint so that there is just enough to produce a strong bond, but no more. Of course this is impossible. You work too fast to be that exact. So to be sure that you have enough glue in the joint, you err on the generous side.

Making Glue Reservoirs

One of the best ways to avoid glue squeeze-out is to cut cavities into the joint where the excess glue can collect, as shown in *Allowing for Excess Glue*. This gives you some leeway in how much glue you can apply without squeeze-out.

Peeling Away Squeeze-Out

Sometimes your reservoirs may not be enough to hold all the excess glue. And sometimes you may

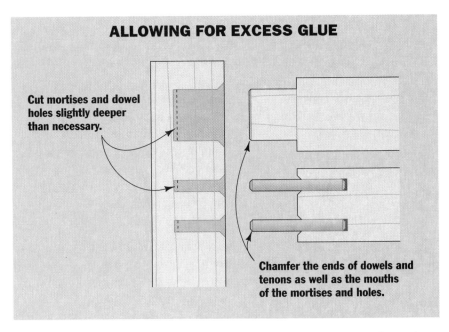

ALLOWING FOR EXCESS GLUE

Cut mortises and dowel holes slightly deeper than necessary.

Chamfer the ends of dowels and tenons as well as the mouths of the mortises and holes.

actually want a bit of squeeze-out to prove that you used enough glue and have tightened the clamps sufficiently (when you're joining boards edge to edge, for example). In these situations, you're faced with a choice as to how to get rid of the excess. One method is to let this seepage tack up and then peel it off. Get the peeling started by sliding a putty knife or dull chisel under the somewhat-hardened glue. Hold the lifted glue between your fingers and lift it away from the wood as you slide the putty knife or

chisel along the joint, as shown in the photo below.

The seepage can also be removed with a wet cloth before it begins to set up. Once the glue has hardened, however, the only way to remove it is to sand or scrape it off the wood. Glue squeeze-out along edge joints is seldom a problem, because you typically sand through all the glue penetration while leveling the surface. But for joints where boards meet perpendicular to each other, sanding can be difficult because of the different grain directions.

It takes a little practice to learn exactly how long to let glue sit (usually 30 minutes to an hour) before peeling it away from a joint.

FACT OR FICTION

DON'T WASTE GLUE ON SHOULDERS

It is not necessary to apply glue to the shoulders of mortise-and-tenon and dowel joints. In fact, it does no good and causes glue-seepage problems. If it were possible to achieve a strong bond by gluing end grain, you wouldn't have to go to the trouble of making joints.

Problem Solving
Gluing and Putting

Glue and wood putty are among the simplest compounds in the workshop, but both are prone to glitches. Here are remedies for common problems.

PROBLEM	SOLUTION
I sanded off the glue that had seeped from one of my mortise-and-tenon joints, but the wood still appears lighter in this area under the stain.	You probably didn't remove all the glue from the wood. Repeat the sanding step one more time, even though the wood is already stained. Just sand through the stain and keep sanding. To ensure that the restaining is even, sand the entire part (rail, stile, leg, or whatever), not just the lighter area. Instead of sanding, you could switch to using paint stripper. Paint stripper removes glue just as it does finish, so it should solve the problem. If the stripper contains wax (most do), wash it off with paint thinner or soap and water. Then resand. You may not need to sand with anything coarser than your final-grit sandpaper.
I tried to even the color on a rail of my cherry table, but the rail is still blotchy.	If you suspect that the blotching stems from a glue seepage problem, strip off as much of the stain as you can using paint stripper, then sand the wood and restain. You don't need to sand all the stain out of the wood before restaining, but you will probably have to strip the entire table to get the overall color even. If the stripper you are using contains wax, be sure to wash all the wax off the surface before restaining. Note that the problem may be the wood itself. Cherry typically blotches. See the solution in "Controlling Blotching" on page 66.
I tried to fill a knothole with wood putty. The putty took a long time to get hard, then cracked. Should I just fill the cracks with more putty?	Yes, fill the cracks once you're sure the original wood putty is completely hardened. But to fill large holes or gouges without cracking, it's best to apply the putty a little at a time. Fill the depression partway, let the putty cure, then continue. When you try doing it all at once, the wood putty takes a very long time to harden all the way through, and it often cracks.
I was a little sloppy with my wood putty. Now that I've applied the stain, there is a light place wherever I got putty onto the wood.	The binder in wood putty is finish, glue, or plaster. It bonds to any wood it comes in contact with, preventing stain penetration. You will have to sand, scrape, or dissolve the putty off the wood and restain. Follow the directions for removing dried glue seepage in "Dealing with Glue Seepage" on page 12.
I washed off all the glue seepage on some doors that I made, but when I stained them, these areas came out darker.	The water raised the grain of the wood, roughening it so that it absorbed more stain. You should have sanded out the roughness before you applied the stain. To sand the doors properly, first remove as much of the stain as you can with paint stripper, then sand to below any color difference and restain.

Dealing with Glue Seepage

Despite your best efforts, you will still have glue seepage now and then (probably a good bit more often than you'd like). You have to remove all the glue from the wood surface, or it will cause color problems after you apply a stain and finish.

Glue is easy to remove while it is still wet. Since most woodworking glues are water-based, simply wash the glue off with water. What you are really doing is thinning the glue with the water and then removing the excess, so it's best to wash the wood several

times to be sure that you have removed as much of the glue as possible from the wood's pores.

It's when the glue hardens that removal presents problems. There are only two ways to remove hardened glue, and they are very logical—scrape and/or sand it off, or dissolve or soften the glue enough so it can be scrubbed off.

Mechanical Removal

Scraping and sanding are pretty straightforward. You need to remove the wood to below where the glue has penetrated and then resand the wood to the same grit you have used elsewhere to ensure that the stain colors the wood evenly.

Solvent Removal

You can soften white and yellow glues enough so that they can be scrubbed off by washing with water. Water works better if it is hot, and still better if you add a little vinegar to it. (Acids soften white and yellow glues, and vinegar is a mild acid.)

A number of commonly available organic solvents can also be used to soften white and yellow glues. In decreasing order of effectiveness these include toluene (toluol), xylene (xylol), acetone, and lacquer thinner. These solvents won't raise the grain of the wood as water does. But water is much more benign and doesn't require a trip to the hardware store.

RIPPINGS

HIGHLIGHTING GLUE SEEPAGE

You'll have an easier time removing glue seepage if you can see the excess glue clearly. The simplest method is to highlight it by wetting the entire surface with water or paint thinner. The liquid will soak deeper into the wood surrounding the glue, leaving the areas that are sealed with glue a lighter color. If you use water to highlight glue seepage, allow the wood to dry and then sand it smooth again because the water will have raised the grain.

Another method of highlighting seepage is to add dye or a proprietary ultraviolet colorant to the glue. The colorant (available from Spotlight 1-800-933-7963) glows when exposed to UV light, making it very easy to spot the smallest trace of wayward glue.

Highlight glue seepage by wetting the surface with water or paint thinner. The liquid will make the glue easier to see.

Whichever liquid you use, you will probably have to scrub a little to get the glue out of the pores. A toothbrush is often enough to get the job done, but sometimes you will need to use a soft, brass-bristled wire brush. These brushes are available at paint stores. After cleaning all the glue out of the pores, sand the wood thoroughly to smooth any roughened grain. You can use a coarser grit of sandpaper, if necessary, but be sure to finish with the same-grit sandpaper as you used on the rest of the piece so the stain colors evenly.

Other glues, like contact cement, can also often be softened or dissolved with solvents. But there are some, like epoxy, that won't soften easily with solvents. With these, you'll have to sand or scrape the glue off the surface.

After Staining

What about glue problems that don't show up until after you have applied a stain? The solution is exactly the same as if you had caught the problem before applying the stain. You still have to remove all the glue, and there are still only two ways to do this: mechanically, or with water or a solvent. How to sand pieces that are already joined together is shown in the sequence, "Sanding Joined Parts."

After removing the glue, you may find that the new application of stain is lighter than the original finish. This is because the stain that remained in the wood acted as a lubricant for the sandpaper, causing it to scratch less deeply. So, even though you may have resanded the surface to exactly the same grit as you used elsewhere, the stain colors a little less.

STEP-BY-STEP: SANDING JOINED PARTS

STEP 1 To sand parts that are joined at a 90-degree angle, sand the butted part first.

STEP 2 Then remove the crossover scratches by sanding the long part.

MASKING TAPE

STEP 3 To sand mitered parts, place masking tape along the edge of one mitered part and sand the other part up to the tape. Then put the tape on the piece you just sanded.

The easy solution to this problem is to apply more stain to the entire part (leg, stile, rail) and resand while the stain is still wet. Then remove the excess stain. The wet sanding will even the scratches over the entire part. If the part is then too light, wet sand again using a coarser-grit sandpaper.

2
CHOOSING FINISHES

Key Ingredients

Paint stores and home centers have a large, often bewildering, number of finishes to choose among, as shown in the photo. What you have to keep in mind is that each finish will perform well in some situations and poorly in others. There is no best finish for all jobs. You can make your choice significantly easier by having a clear idea of each product's most important qualities:

● How well the finish protects the wood
● How durable the finish is
● How easy the finish is to apply

Protection

The primary protective purpose of a finish is to reduce stresses in joints by slowing moisture-vapor exchange in and out of the wood. When the air is humid, wood absorbs moisture and expands. When the air is dry, the wood releases moisture and shrinks. It is important to note that expansion and shrinkage occur only in one direction, across the grain. Wood doesn't expand or shrink significantly along the grain. It is this difference that causes trouble, as shown in *Wood Movement.*

When you join pieces of wood with the grain running in opposite directions, as you almost always do

It is easy to be confused by the large number of finishes on the market. To make sense out of the choices, learn the characteristics of each type of finish (oil, varnish, shellac, lacquer, water-base). Then pick the finish that will give you the characteristics you want most.

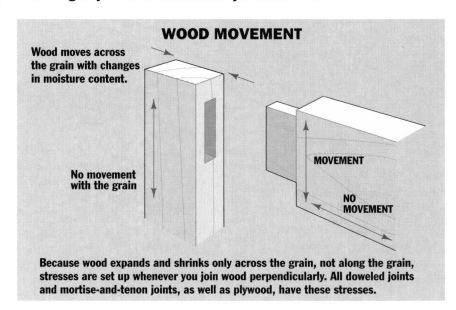

WOOD MOVEMENT

Wood moves across the grain with changes in moisture content.

No movement with the grain

MOVEMENT

NO MOVEMENT

Because wood expands and shrinks only across the grain, not along the grain, stresses are set up whenever you join wood perpendicularly. All doweled joints and mortise-and-tenon joints, as well as plywood, have these stresses.

when making useful objects, you build in stresses that will eventually loosen the joints. By applying a finish, you can minimize the damaging effects of this expansion-contraction cycle on woodworking projects.

Even veneered plywood and veneered manufactured board (particleboard and medium-density fiberboard, commonly abbreviated MDF) have their built-in stresses. The plies in plywood run in opposite directions. The veneer on stable manufactured board shrinks and expands while the substrate does not. (The only exceptions to cross-grain stresses are single piece objects like turnings and carvings.)

If you want your project to have the greatest chance for long life, you should choose a finish that offers maximum resistance to moisture-vapor exchange, as shown in *Resisting Moisture.* Within each finish type (oil, varnish, shellac, lacquer, and water-based), the

thicker the finish coat, the better it slows this exchange.

There is a limit to thickness, however. Film thicknesses greater than about 0.006 inch (four coats of polyurethane or so) have a tendency to crack, especially if the weather goes through sudden, radical changes. In addition to detracting visually, cracks offset the protective qualities of the film because they allow moisture through.

Durability

Durability is the degree to which the finish film resists damage. Some finishes resist scratches, water, solvents, heat, and household chemicals better than others. For a decorative object that will sit on a fireplace mantel all its life, finish durability is not very important. But for a vanity, tabletop, or set of kitchen cabinets, finish durability is crucial in handling abuse.

Finish durability depends less on thickness than on the type of finish itself. But, within each finish type, the thicker the finish film, the longer it will survive wear and tear.

Ease of Application

The most important factor for ease of applying a finish is speed of drying. This may surprise you until you recall the problems you've had with dust getting into slow-drying finishes like polyurethane. The problem with choosing a fast-drying finish is that the faster it dries, the more difficult it is to apply with a rag or brush. You're almost forced to use a spray gun. And if you don't have one, you often can't use that finish.

The exception is when you wipe off all the excess finish after each coat. In this case, you don't have to worry about dust because there isn't enough finish left on the surface for it to stick to.

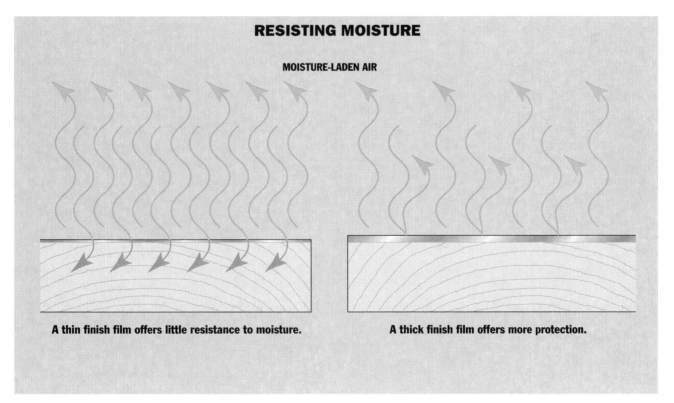

RESISTING MOISTURE

MOISTURE-LADEN AIR

A thin finish film offers little resistance to moisture.   A thick finish film offers more protection.

Sealing Wood

There is probably no area of finishing more confusing than sealing wood. Instructions in books and magazines commonly recommend sealing wood before applying a finish. Paint stores sell special products called "sealers." Some finishes are touted as "self-sealing." Yet *all* finishes are self-sealing, and there is no product better at sealing wood than a common finish. Thus, no separate product is needed to seal wood under a finish.

The problem here is largely one of language. "Sealers" are mis-named. "Self-sealing" is misused. To understand what is going on, think of pores in wood as strawlike holes going down into the wood. When you put a coat of finish onto wood, the finish runs down into the pores, cures, and stops the pores up, as shown in *What Sealers Do*. Thus, the first coat of any finish "seals" the wood and is therefore,

by definition, the "sealer" coat. All subsequent coats of finish are "top coats." They build on top of a sealed wood surface.

But the first coat of finish causes the wood to feel rough, even if you sanded the wood well first. The finish encases raised wood fibers that you may not have

noticed before, because they were soft. Sanding this surface level is often difficult, especially with finishes like varnish and lacquer, which tend to gum up sandpaper. So, manufacturers make "sanding sealers" as first coats that can be easily sanded.

Sanding Sealers

Sanding sealers are usually a mixture of the regular finish—varnish, lacquer, or water-based finish—and a soaplike lubricant. "Sanding sealer" describes these products well, but they are commonly referred to (and sometimes labeled as) simply "sealers," and this causes confusion.

The purpose of a sanding sealer is to make smoothing the first coat of finish easier, as shown in the top photo on the opposite page. When you use a sanding sealer as the first coat, it is also the sealer coat. If you apply a second coat of sanding sealer (to give yourself a thicker cushion so you are less likely to sand through), it is technically a top coat. This second coat of sanding sealer can't be considered another sealer coat because the wood has already been sealed by the first coat.

Sanding sealers are especially suited to saving time in production situations where a large surface area has to be sanded after the first coat. But if you are finishing a small project, speed is seldom so important. You can apply the finish itself as the first coat and then just take a little longer to do the sanding. Or you can achieve almost the same degree of easy sanding by thinning the first coat of finish by about half with the appropriate thinner. This makes the resulting film thinner, so it cures harder faster, making sanding easier. (This is the correct rationale for

WHAT SEALERS DO

Sealers stop up the pores in the wood's surface so other liquids cannot penetrate.

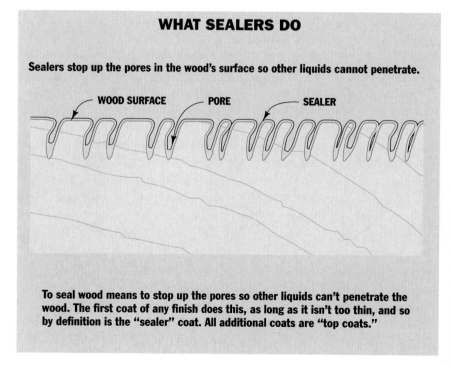

WOOD SURFACE   PORE   SEALER

To seal wood means to stop up the pores so other liquids can't penetrate the wood. The first coat of any finish does this, as long as it isn't too thin, and so by definition is the "sealer" coat. All additional coats are "top coats."

thinning the first coat of finish, not for achieving a better bond to the wood, as is often stated.)

Sanding sealers can also be used to partially fill pores. Though the effect is not easily apparent to an untrained eye, the soaplike particles in sanding sealer produce a little more pore filling than the finish itself. Some finishers use sanding sealers to create a more level surface on woods like maple, cherry, walnut, and mahogany.

Weaknesses of Sanding Sealers

Sanding sealers are less protective and durable than their corresponding finish. Being a soap-type product, the lubricant absorbs moisture, making sanding sealers weak moisture barriers. In addition, the quality that makes these products easy to sand also renders them easy to scratch and fracture, as shown in the photo at right. So sanding sealers shouldn't be applied thicker than necessary for sanding or mild filling. And they should never be used as a final finish.

Sanding sealers combine a soaplike lubricant with a finish to make sanding easier; the finish powders easily when sanded, and this keeps sandpaper from clogging.

A sanding sealer will weaken the finish when it is applied thick. The soaplike lubricant breaks apart easily if the surface of the finish receives a sharp blow, as when these keys were dropped on a tabletop.

SEALERS AND PRIMERS

Part of the confusion about sealers is that they are thought of as equivalents to primers for paint. The assumption is that because a primer should be used under paint, a sealer is required under a finish. But this is not true. Primers and sealers perform entirely different functions.

Primers are necessary because paint won't bond well to bare wood by itself. Paint contains a high percentage of pigment (in order to cover better) and only enough binder to glue the pigment particles to each other and to an underlying smooth surface. Since wood is porous, and thus not smooth, more binder is required to achieve a good bond. Paint primer therefore contains a higher binder-to-pigment ratio than paint. Primer provides a smooth surface for subsequent coats of paint to bond to. Primer also covers less well than paint because it contains less pigment.

Unlike paint, finishes bond well to wood since they are essentially pure binder. A sanding sealer does nothing to improve this bond. On the contrary, sanding sealers actually weaken the bond of the finish to the wood, because their soaplike lubricant reduces the ability of a finish to flow out and fully wet the surface. Without complete wetting, complete bonding is impossible.

Oil Finishes

There are two types of oil: those that cure, and those that don't. Oils that cure can be used as finishes since they seal the wood and produce a fairly permanent sheen. Oils that don't cure don't perform well as finishes because either they continue to soak deeper into the wood, leaving the surface unprotected, or they remain sticky on the surface.

Common examples of oils that don't cure are mineral oil, vegetable oil, lubricating oil, and motor oil. There are two commonly available oils that cure and thus perform well as finishes: linseed oil and pure tung oil, shown in the photo at right.

Linseed oil is pressed from the seeds of the flax plant. Its slow curing time—a week or longer—makes raw linseed oil very impractical to use as a finish. Manufacturers add metallic dryers to speed the curing to

Two natural oils, boiled linseed oil and pure tung oil, can be used successfully as finishes because both cure, meaning they turn from a liquid to a solid.

about a day. This product is called "boiled linseed oil," even though it is not actually boiled. For the most part, when woodworkers talk about "linseed oil," they are actually referring to boiled linseed oil.

Tung oil is pressed from the nuts of the tung tree, which is native to China. The pure tung oil sold in the United States as a wood finish does not have dryers added, and it takes two or three days to cure when all the excess is wiped off the wood. Pure tung oil thus cures faster than raw linseed oil but more slowly than boiled linseed oil.

Neither linseed oil nor tung oil is very protective, because neither can be built up significantly. Both oils cure soft and wrinkled, as shown in the photo at left, so all the excess should be wiped off after each coat. Otherwise, the film that is left will scratch easily and be sticky in humid weather. Good durability is not possible either, because neither oil cures hard enough to resist wear.

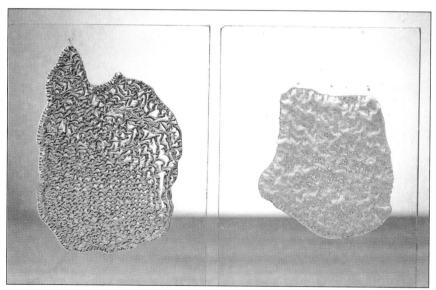

When raw or boiled linseed oil (left) and pure tung oil (right) are applied thick to a surface, they take months to cure. And even then they will be soft and wrinkled, as is evident in these samples applied to glass. Because of the extremely slow curing and the softness of the cured film, all the excess of these oils should be wiped off after each coat.

Relatively speaking, however, pure tung oil is slightly more protective and durable than boiled linseed oil. Both oils are easy to apply, and this is the main reason they are popular.

The thinner for linseed oil and tung oil is turpentine or paint thinner (mineral spirits). Any amount of thinner can be added to these oils, but the only benefit is easier application. The thinner a liquid, the easier it is to wipe or brush over a surface. Thinness doesn't have any significant effect on the depth to which an oil will penetrate. Penetration is controlled primarily by how long the oil stays wet on the surface and if the oil can find a passage deeper into the wood, as shown in the photo. The only effect thinning has on penetration is that it speeds it up initially.

A liquid will penetrate all the way through wood if it stays wet long enough and if it can find a way. Because both linseed oil and tung oil cure very slowly, they penetrate deeply into wood if they are kept wet on the surface. There is no need to thin the oil to get it to penetrate. Here, boiled linseed oil has penetrated all the way through the end grain of a maple dowel.

FACT OR FICTION

MYTHS ABOUT LINSEED AND PURE TUNG OILS

● MYTH: Multiple coats of linseed oil will create one of the most water resistant finishes in existence.

In fact, a linseed oil finish is one of the least water resistant of all finishes. This is true no matter how the oil is applied, how many coats are applied, or how long it has cured.

● MYTH: Pure tung oil is so water resistant that it was once used to protect the Great Wall of China.

This is ridiculous. How can an oil, which breaks down quickly in sunlight and rain, be effective at protecting rock? How many nuts from tung trees would it take to create enough oil to coat such a large structure, said to be the only man-made object that can be seen from space?

● MYTH: Oil finishes that contain metallic dryers are unsafe for use on objects that may come in contact with food, or that may be chewed on by children.

In fact, the Food and Drug Administration (FDA) approves the use of all common metallic dryers (lead is not allowed and is not used) in oil and varnish finishes. No commonly available finish, including oils with dryers added, is unsafe for food contact once the finish has thoroughly cured.

● MYTH:Rubbing or heating an oil finish increases penetration.

As explained in the text, oils penetrate perfectly well without additional manipulation. But if you think about it, rubbing or heating the oil actually makes it cure faster, which causes it to stop up the pores sooner and thus decreases rather than increases penetration.

Varnishes and Wiping Varnish

Varnish is made by cooking an oil, such as linseed oil, tung oil, or modified soybean oil, with a resin. Natural resins such as copol, kauri, and amber, which are fossilized sap, were once used. The resins used in varnishes today are synthetic alkyds, phenolics, and polyurethanes, and the name on the can indicates what you're getting, as shown in the photo. Of these, varnishes made with polyurethane resin are the most commonly available and the most popular. These products are usually referred to simply as "polyurethane," but in fact they are a type of varnish. The polyurethane resins make this type of varnish a little more protective and durable than the others.

When more oil and less resin is used in the manufacture, the resulting varnish is softer and more flexible. This type of varnish, usually called "spar" varnish, is best for exterior use because it flexes to accommodate the greater wood movement outdoors. The best spar varnishes are made with tung oil and phenolic resin because these ingredients combine to produce the best water resistance.

Varnish comes in sheens that range from gloss to flat. Satin is probably the most popular sheen, because it imitates the appearance of a finish rubbed with steel wool. Since the flatting agent that creates the satin sheen settles to the bottom of the can, you should stir this type of varnish before using it.

Varnish is one of the most protective and durable of all finishes. Of course, three or four coats are more protective and durable than one or two. But varnish can be problematic to apply. Because it cures so slowly, dust has a lot of time to settle and stick to the finish.

Wiping Varnish

Varnish can be thinned with any amount of paint thinner (mineral spirits). When varnish is thinned by about half with paint thinner, it becomes easy to wipe on wood and is called "wiping varnish." Wiping varnishes are widely available.

Unfortunately, many manufacturers label their wiping varnish "tung oil," or imply in their marketing that the finish is tung oil or some other type of oil, and this causes confusion.

In fact, varnish and tung oil are two entirely different finishes. When left thick on a surface, tung oil takes months to cure to a soft wrinkled film. When an oil is combined with a resin and cooked, the resulting varnish cures overnight to a hard smooth film. To make matters even more confusing, most of the wiping varnishes that are sold as "tung" oil aren't even made with tung oil. They are made with modified soybean oil and alkyd resin.

Manufacturers cause tremendous problems for the craft by misrepresenting their products. The burden then falls on you to figure out which product you're using. You can't rely on the name or description on the container. You will need to test any product that claims to be tung oil to see what you really have, as shown in the photo on the opposite page.

Wiping varnish provides excellent protection and durability, just like full-strength varnish. But it

Three broad categories of varnish can be identified by the name on the can. "Varnish" usually means an alkyd-resin varnish that cures relatively hard. "Spar varnish" means a varnish that cures relatively soft and flexible; phenolic resin is usually used. "Polyurethane" means a varnish that is relatively more durable.

takes many more coats to achieve the same thickness. Also, just like full-strength varnish, wiping varnish cures slowly, so dust is a problem if you don't wipe off all the excess varnish after each coat.

RIPPINGS

STORING VARNISH

After you have used part of a can of varnish or wiping varnish, storing the rest is troublesome because there is often enough air in the top of the container to cause the varnish to skin over. You sometimes hear of putting marbles into the container to fill up the air space. Though this practice works, it wastes marbles and you risk contaminating the finish with dirt. A better and simpler solution is to pour the varnish over into a smaller container—usually a jar with a tight fitting lid.

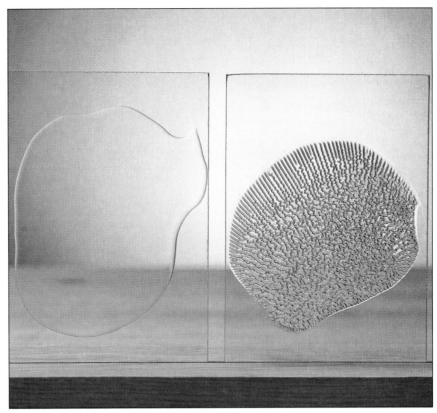

To test if a finish is wiping varnish or tung oil, pour some onto glass and let it cure overnight. If it cures hard and smooth, it is wiping varnish. If it doesn't cure at all, it is tung oil. If it cures soft and wrinkled, it is a mixture of oil and varnish. See "Oil/Varnish-Blend Finishes" on page 22.

SHOP SOLUTIONS: Making Your Own Wiping Varnish

You can make your own wiping varnish by thinning any varnish or nonwater-based polyurethane with paint thinner (mineral spirits). Begin with a mixture of half varnish (polyurethane) and half thinner, then add more varnish or more thinner to achieve the working qualities you like best. A thicker varnish will build faster, but will be harder to apply. Thinner varnish goes on easily, but requires more coats to reach the same level of protection.

When mixing up your own wiping varnish, start with equal amounts of varnish and paint thinner.

Oil/Varnish-Blend Finishes

Varnish can be mixed with linseed oil or tung oil in any proportion, making a product that is a little more protective and durable than oil alone. But, like oil, this "oil/varnish blend" still cures slowly to a soft, wrinkled film. All the excess finish should be wiped off after each coat, or the film will scratch easily and be sticky in humid weather.

Oil/varnish blends are very popular finishes because they are so easy to use. Most are sold under names like "Danish oil" or "teak oil" to suggest a relationship with the finish used on imported Scandinavian furniture. (This furniture is actually finished with two-part, catalyzed lacquer, not oil.)

Many formulas circulate for

making your own oil/varnish-blend finish. These blends will be similar to popular commercial products, and the ingredients are few, as shown in the photo. The most common of these formulas suggests mixing equal parts of varnish, boiled linseed oil, and turpentine or paint thinner (mineral spirits). The turpentine and paint thinner act to thin the mixture of oil and varnish so it is easier to apply.

This formula can be varied in any way you like. For example, you can substitute tung oil (which is slightly more durable, expensive, and produces a slightly duller sheen) for boiled linseed oil, or use some of both oils. You can substitute polyurethane (again, for durability's sake) for other types of varnish. You can vary the ratio of oil and varnish, and you can add more or less thinner to achieve the working qualities you like best. The higher the ratio of varnish, the more protective and durable the finish. The higher the ratio of boiled linseed oil, the longer it will take before it begins to set up. The higher the ratio of thinner, the easier the finish will be to apply and the less likely the first coat will seal the wood. Whatever mix you concoct, the level of gloss will remain about the same. Oil/varnish blends always produce a satin sheen.

Note: some recipes suggest adding beeswax to the mixture. Though this can be done, the beeswax will weaken the finish. It will watermark easily and it may be sticky in hot, humid weather. If you want to add wax, use it as a polish, as discussed in "Caring for Furniture" on page 86.

By mixing varnish, boiled linseed oil, and paint thinner, you can make your own version of some very popular "oil" finishes. You can mix the three ingredients in any proportion.

Shellac

Shellac is a natural resin secreted by insects, called lac bugs, which attach themselves to certain trees in and around northern India and Thailand. The resin is scraped from the twigs and branches of the trees, melted and strained to remove bug parts and other foreign matter. The resin is then formed into large sheets that are broken up into flakes and shipped around the world. You can buy shellac in flake form or already dissolved, as shown in the photo at right.

In its natural form, shellac is orange in color and contains about 5 percent wax. The orange color can be used to advantage when you want to add warmth to the wood, as shown in the photo below. But it is a disadvantage if you want to maintain the color of a pickling stain or of light-colored woods, such as maple, birch, or poplar. Therefore, most suppliers provide a bleached shellac that has had the orange color removed. These bleached shellacs are called

Shellac is available in both flakes, to be dissolved in denatured alcohol, and ready to use in already-dissolved form. Both are sold in orange and bleached colors.

"white," "clear," or "super blond" and are virtually colorless, as shown. You can mix orange and bleached shellac to achieve an in-between color.

The naturally occurring wax causes liquid shellac to appear cloudy, and it slightly reduces the transparency and water resistance of the cured film. For most situations where you are using shellac as the entire finish, the wax makes little difference in performance. But it can prevent good bonding when shellac is used under varnish, polyurethane, or water-based finish. Some suppliers remove the wax from the flake form, but all shellac sold already dissolved in cans still contains wax. You can make your own dewaxed shellac from a can of shellac by allowing the wax to settle in the container and then decanting the liquid.

Shellac has a long history, and the system for measuring it is also old. It is based on the term "pound cut" and is an easy system to remember. A 1-pound cut is the ratio of 1 pound of shellac flakes dissolved in 1 gallon of alcohol. Thus, 2 pounds of shellac flakes in 1 gallon of alcohol is a 2-pound cut, and 1 pound of flakes in 1 quart of alcohol is a 4-pound cut. You can

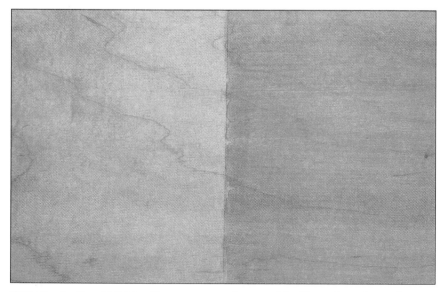

Orange shellac (right) adds a warm amber cast to the color of wood. Bleached shellac adds virtually no color at all.

make up any quantity of liquid shellac at any pound cut simply by keeping this ratio.

Most supplier-dissolved shellac is a 3-pound cut, even if the can doesn't say so. A 3-pound cut is a little thick for brushing and much too thick for spraying. For easy brushing, reduce the 3-pound-cut shellac with nearly an equal amount of denatured alcohol. For easy spraying, reduce 1 part of the 3-pound-cut shellac with 2 parts alcohol. Make adjustments from there to reach the thickness, or pound cut, you feel most comfortable with.

An Underappreciated Finish

Today, shellac is an underappreciated finish. It was once the primary finish used in furniture factories and small woodworking shops. For at least 100 years prior to the 1920s, when lacquer was introduced, almost all high-quality furniture made in the United States and Europe was finished with shellac. Much of this furniture still survives with its original finish intact. Moreover, before the availability of polyurethane, shellac was one of the most popular finishes used on wood trim and floors in houses.

Though shellac is not as protective and durable as varnish, lacquer, and water-based finishes, it performs well enough for most situations. Exceptions include kitchen cabinets and tabletops which are often subjected to rough use. Shellac dries slowly enough so it can be brushed, but fast enough so dust in the air is seldom a serious problem. Shellac can also be combined with a little oil and rubbed on a surface to create an attractive, level film build. This technique is called French polishing. (See French Polishing on page 46.)

SHOP SOLUTIONS: Mixing Your Own Shellac

To dissolve shellac flakes, add enough denatured alcohol (ethyl alcohol that has been made poisonous so it is not taxed as a liquor) to the flakes to make the pound cut you want. Use a jar or other nonmetallic container, as shown, because metal reacts with the shellac and causes it to darken. Keep the jar covered so the alcohol doesn't absorb moisture from the air. Moisture will cause the shellac to blush (turn milky white).

When the flakes are totally in solution, remove impurities by straining the shellac through a paint strainer or loose-weave cheesecloth into another jar, and write the current date on the jar so you know when the shellac was made. (Dissolved shellac starts deteriorating immediately.)

Orange shellac will keep in flake form for many years, but bleached shellac won't. After a short time, usually six months to a year, bleached flakes begin stick-

To make your own shellac from flakes, combine the flakes with denatured alcohol and stir the mixture occasionally until the flakes dissolve (usually in several hours). A good beginning mix is ¼ pound of flakes in 1 pint of alcohol. This makes a 2-pound cut, which is fairly easy to brush.

ing together in a lump, and they no longer dissolve easily. The deterioration continues until the flakes won't dissolve at all. Buy

bleached flakes only as you need them, and test the ability of the dissolved shellac to dry hard before using it.

Shellac, like lacquer, has the advantage that its thinner is also its stripper. So, if you are dissatisfied with a shellac finish, you can easily wash it away with some denatured alcohol and start over.

Also important in this era of concern for health and the environment, the denatured-alcohol solvent used in shellac is relatively benign. There is very little stink, and as long as you use denatured ethyl alcohol (also sold as shellac thinner) and not methyl alcohol (methanol), which is quite toxic, inhaling the fumes is not particularly harmful. Nevertheless, as when using any finish, you should still arrange cross ventilation in your finishing area to protect yourself. Shellac is not listed as a pollutant or ozone-depleting solvent by the Environmental Protection Agency (EPA).

TROUBLESHOOTING

SHELLAC'S SHELF LIFE

Many people have had a bad experience using shellac because it dried slowly or never hardened. The shellac was too old.

Shellac's biggest disadvantage is that it has a short shelf life. It begins to deteriorate as soon as it is dissolved in alcohol. This is true whether you do the dissolving yourself or the supplier does it, and it occurs even if the shellac is kept in a sealed container. The deterioration occurs slowly. You won't notice it for six months to a year. But then you can begin to tell that the shellac dries more slowly, and that it never gets as hard. Suppliers of shellac have differing interpretations of adequate hardness and drying time, and they often list this interpretation on their containers along with a date of manufacture. Some suppliers don't date their containers at all.

You should always use the freshest shellac you can get, because it will perform better. If you dissolve your own, date the container so you know when you made it. If you buy shellac already dissolved, find a store that carries dated cans, and pick those with the most recent date of manufacture.

To determine if shellac is still all right to use, pour some out of the can onto a piece of glass or other nonporous surface. Give the shellac several seconds to spread out. Then tilt the glass to almost vertical, and let the shellac run down the glass and off the bottom, as shown below. The objective is to get a uniformly thin layer of shellac. Lean the glass against a stationary object and let the shellac dry for about an hour at room temperature. The shellac should be hard enough at this point so it doesn't show the impression of a fingerprint. After drying overnight, the shellac should be hard enough so you can't indent it with your fingernail.

Alternatively, apply three coats of shellac that has been thinned to a 2-pound-cut to a piece of scrap wood within an eight-hour period, let the shellac dry overnight, then check to see if it is hard.

To test shellac to make sure it will dry, apply a thin coat to a nonporous surface. After the shellac dries overnight, you shouldn't be able to indent it with your fingernail.

Lacquer

There are two commonly available lacquers: nitrocellulose, and CAB-acrylic (also called water-white). Nitrocellulose lacquer has been the most widely used finish in furniture factories and professional refinishing shops for the last 70 years. CAB-acrylic is not quite as durable, but it doesn't yellow as much, so it is used in situations where minimum yellowing is desired. Both lacquers act almost identically in application. Both are more protective and durable than shellac, roughly the same as water-based finishes, and less so than varnish.

The primary reason for the popularity of lacquer is its versatility when applied with a spray gun. Lacquer makes the finisher's job easier. Among the qualities finishers like are the following:

● Reduced runs and sags on vertical surfaces. Lacquer stays put on vertical surfaces better than any other finish because of the quick evaporation rate of lacquer thinner.
● Ease of achieving dust-free, blush-free, and overspray-free application in all types of weather. There are lacquer thinners available that evaporate fast or slow so the drying speed of the lacquer can be controlled no matter what the weather conditions, as shown in the photo.
● Problem-free results when used in combination with stains, glazes, and paste-wood fillers. Lacquer is compatible with all these decorative products as long as enough time is allowed for them to cure and the first

couple of coats are not applied heavily.
● Ease of use as a toner. Lacquer is the only finish, other than shellac, that dries fast enough and can be thinned enough so that it can be used as a toner. (A toner is made by combining about 1 part stain with about 1 part finish, and thinning with 6 or more parts thinner. It is used to shade or tone the wood to a slightly different color.)
● Ease of repair. Lacquer is the only finish, other than shellac, that can be dissolved with heat or solvent so that more finish can be blended into a damaged area of the existing finish.
● Superior rubbing qualities. Lacquer cures hard and brittle enough so that abrasives can be used to rub an even sheen. No

other finish rubs as easily or to as pleasing a result.
● Relative ease of stripping. Lacquer is the only finish, other than shellac, that can be washed off wood with its own thinner (lacquer thinner). All other finishes require stronger finish removers.

Lacquer Thinner

The vehicle for lacquer, called "lacquer thinner," is responsible for much of the versatility in application. But lacquer thinner is also highly toxic and highly flammable, and it is polluting to the atmosphere. To make matters worse, it takes a high percentage of lacquer thinner (up to 85 percent) to make lacquer sprayable.

Because of the toxicity and flammability, you should never

Thinners are available to modify the way lacquer behaves. In cold weather, when lacquer would normally cure very slowly, it can be made to cure faster so dust doesn't have time to settle. In humid weather, when blushing is a problem, the lacquer can be made to cure more slowly so moisture has time to evaporate out of the lacquer before it cures. In hot weather, when lacquer cures too fast, it can be made to cure more slowly so that overspray still melts back in when it falls back on the lacquer surface.

spray lacquer in a room that doesn't have adequate and safe ventilation. Because of concern over air quality, in some parts of the country the use of lacquer may be regulated in factories and large shops.

Lacquer is usually sprayed, but it can also be brushed, as shown in the photo at right. To make a brushing lacquer, manufacturers dissolve the lacquer in a slow-evaporating lacquer thinner. This provides the time necessary for the lacquer to be brushed out on a surface. Working with a brushing lacquer is very much like working with shellac. The advantage of brushing lacquer over shellac is that you have fewer problems with dust. The disadvantage of using brushing lacquer is that you have to work faster.

Lacquer is usually thought of as a spraying finish, but specially made lacquers dry slowly enough that they can be brushed. Lacquer is also sometimes wiped on wood with a rag by woodturners working on a lathe.

FINISHING SAFETY

Like woodworking, wood finishing has its inherent dangers. The solvents and other chemicals used in finishing can be potentially harmful and should be treated with respect.

The danger from finishing comes from contact with the chemicals you're using, especially the solvents that many finishes contain. To protect yourself from direct contact, wear gloves as you're working. But beware, not all gloves offer adequate protection. Latex dishwashing gloves will keep your hands clean, but may allow the solvents through. For the best protection, get nitrile latex gloves (available from Conney Safety Products, 1-800-356-9100).

For protection from fumes, keep your work space well ventilated. This means more than simply opening a window; you need cross ventilation to provide a constant supply of fresh air. Set up fans, if necessary, to keep the air moving. (Be sure to use explosion-proof models if you're using fans to exhaust solvent fumes.) If you're spraying, you'll also need a respirator in addition to good ventilation. Get a snug fitting one with organic vapor cartridges. For sanding and rubbing out between coats, a heavy-duty dust mask is in order. Get masks that are OSHA approved for filtering wood dust. The light-duty masks sold at most stores offer little real protection.

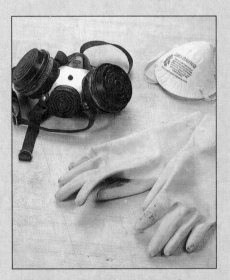

Finishing safely doesn't require a lot of equipment. A respirator with organic vapor cartridges for fumes, a mask for dust, and gloves to protect your hands will cover most situations.

Water-Based Finish

Because of stricter air-quality laws in some parts of the country, a market has been created for water-based finishes. These finishes are often marketed as "varnish," "polyurethane," or "lacquer," which confuses them with solvent-based products of the same names. But water-based finishes are always identifiable by some mention of water cleanup on the can. Though water-based finishes still do contain organic solvents, they use less than most other finishes.

The only significant difference between brands of water-based finishes is the resin used. Some water-based finishes are made with acrylic resin, some with polyurethane resin, and some with a combination of acrylic and polyurethane resins. These vary somewhat in durability, especially in toughness (polyurethane is more scratch resistant) and in color (acrylic is totally non-yellowing while

Water-based finishes don't level well, so significant sanding is often required to produce a flat, level surface.

polyurethane yellows a little). But there are no significant differences in protection or ease of application.

Water-based finishes are more complex to produce than either lacquer or varnish, and they are more expensive. Latex paint and white and yellow glue are familiar products that make use of the same technology. In fact, the easiest way to understand water-based finishes is to think of them as latex paint without the pigment.

Water-based finishes are much closer to latex paint without the pigment (and to white and yellow glue) than they are to the solvent-based finishes that share the same names. They use the same technology as water-based paint and have many of the same advantages and disadvantages.

Advantages and Limitations

Water-based finishes have many of the same good and bad qualities as latex paint. The most important benefits are reduced solvent smell and easy brush cleanup. Relatively fast curing also reduces dust problems. It is these qualities that will, in time, make water-based finishes just as popular with recreational woodworkers as latex paint is with homeowners.

The significant limitations of water-based finishes are pronounced brush marking (shown in the photo above) and reduced durability. Compared to oil-based varnishes and polyurethanes, water-based finishes level poorly and are much less resistant to damage from heat, solvents, acids, and alkalies. They are slightly more resistant to these elements, however, than shellac and lacquer.

In addition, water-based finishes bubble at least as badly as oil-based varnishes when they are brushed, and the bubbles are less likely to pop out before the finish cures. Adding water to the finish seldom helps. Some manufacturers supply a solvent that reduces bubbling and

TROUBLESHOOTING

GRAIN-RAISING REMEDIES

Whenever you put water on wood, the wood will feel rough, no matter how well you sanded it. This roughness is called "raised grain," and there are several ways you can handle it.

● Raise the grain and sand it level before you apply the finish. This is called "sponging" or "dewhiskering." First, wipe over the wood with a wet rag or sponge. Allow the wood to dry overnight, then sand it with sandpaper of a grit that removes the roughness efficiently without cutting significantly deeper into the wood. Cutting deeper exposes fresh wood that will raise again when water is applied. The appropriate sandpaper grits are usually between 220 and 400.

● Wipe or brush the first coat of water-based finish onto the wood and scuff the wood with synthetic Scotch-Brite pads

Wetting a piece of sanded wood will inevitably raise little whiskers on the surface. These must be sanded away at some point to produce an attractive level surface.

before the finish cures. Let the finish cure, then continue with additional coats. Don't use steel wool for this step—any leftover pieces will cause rust marks

under the finish.

● Apply the first coat of water-based finish. Let it cure. Then sand it level, just as you normally would do after the first coat of finish.

● Apply a sealer coat that doesn't raise the grain. This could be any finish except shellac that contains wax. Water-based finish doesn't bond well to waxed shellac. Applying water-based finish over another finish is equivalent to applying latex paint over shellac, lacquer, varnish, or oil paint. People do it all the time with good results, as long as the underlying surface is clean and dull. If you use another finish as a sealer coat under a water-based finish, you must be sure that that coat is fully cured. You may also want to question your purpose in using a water-based finish. If you are willing to use a solvent-based finish for the sealer coat, why not continue to use it for the top coats?

improves flow out, but few stores stock it. Adding a solvent is problematic anyway, because it defeats the primary rationale for using a water-based finish—getting away from the use of solvents.

One quality that can be either positive or negative depending on the effect you want is color. Water-based finishes have almost no color as shown in the photo at right. This produces a washed-out look on darker woods like walnut, but causes no yellowing on lighter woods like maple, or over white pickling. To achieve the darkening familiar with solvent-based finishes, use a stain.

Many familiar solvent-based finishes impart a warm amber color to the wood underneath (lower half, both samples). Water-based finishes (upper half, both samples) add virtually no color. This lack of color can work for or against you depending on the look you're after.

Choosing a Finish

It is one thing to list the relative merits of various finishes. It is another to actually apply the information to real-world choices. Here are a number of common examples of finishing projects and the thought process you may want to use in choosing a finish.

Kitchen Cabinets The main quality you want in a finish for kitchen (or bathroom) cabinets is durability. The finish should be wear resistant and able to resist damage from frequent contact with acids in body oils and alkalies in soaps. Hands transfer these acids and alkalies, causing finishes to soften and darken around knobs and pulls over time. Given these needs, varnish or polyurethane is clearly the best choice. If you want to wipe on the finish rather than brush it on, thin the finish to make a wiping varnish.

If the solvent smell of varnish and polyurethane is more than you would like in your house, or if you can't keep the air in your finishing area clear of dust, you could choose a water-based finish. You will get almost the same wear resistance with fewer dust and odor problems.

Lacquer is also an acceptable alternative; in fact it is the most common finish used by professionals when finishing cabinets on location. Shellac and oil finishes will give very poor performance. Cabinets that are prefinished in factories almost always have a two-part catalyzed finish, combining the durability of polyurethane with the fast drying quality of lacquer.

Dining Tables and Chairs Your choice for these items will hinge around the look and durability you

Kitchen and bathroom cabinets are apt to see hard use, so a durable finish is in order unless you want to spend a lot of time on upkeep. Polyurethane varnish will give the longest-lasting results.

want for the most important surface, the tabletop. For wear, you should choose a film-building finish. For looks, you will need to decide if you want to rub out the finish. Lacquer rubs most easily, shellac next. Varnishes and water-based finishes

can be rubbed fairly successfully, but only to a satin sheen—about what is produced by #0000 steel wool. It is difficult to keep streaks out when rubbing to a higher gloss.

Coffee and End Tables Any of the finishes could be used success-

Base your finish choice on the surface that will receive the most abuse. In the case of a dining suite, that surface is the tabletop.

fully on coffee and end tables. But you will get better wear from a finish that can be built up to a thicker film than you will from an oil finish. Of the film finishes, varnish, polyurethane, and water-based provide the best scratch resistance. In making your choice you should take into consideration the care with which the tables will be treated. To get really first-class results, consider rubbing out the tabletop.

Book Shelves and Entertainment Centers These objects generally don't get a lot of wear. Appearance is usually more important. Other than orange shellac, which will warm the wood, and water-based finish, which won't add any color, the principal quality that makes finishes look different is how thick they are applied. Oil, oil/varnish blends, and wiping varnish are easy to apply very thin. You can apply any other finish over these if you decide you want more thickness, as long as you let the first coat cure thoroughly first.

RIPPINGS

SANDING SEALERS

Sanding sealers cure faster than their corresponding finish, and they make sanding easier. They are also somewhat better at pore filling than the finish itself. But a finish with a sanding sealer that is used as an undercoat isn't as strong as one without. Sanding sealers decrease a finish's moisture resistance, scratch easier than their corresponding finish, fracture when struck if they are applied thick, and can cause the finish to bond so poorly that it peels at the sanding sealer/finish interface.

My advice is to stay away from sanding sealers unless you are finishing large surfaces that can be difficult to sand, are in a hurry, or want the extra pore-filling capability.

Small Boxes Like Those for Jewelry These tend to be well cared for and treated more like decorative objects, even though they may also serve a functional purpose. Thin, close-to-the-wood finishes seem to be the most popular for these objects. Therefore, you will probably choose between an oil/varnish blend and a wiping varnish, depending on the gloss you want. A gloss wiping varnish will produce a higher gloss than an oil/varnish blend. If you want a high gloss you could French polish the object with shellac. If you have spray equipment, you might choose to spray lacquer.

Decorative Turnings and Carvings These objects generally don't receive any wear, and because there are no joints, protection is of less significance. Appearance and ease of application are most important.

In most cases a thin finish looks best, so choose one of the finishes that is easy to wipe on, considering both sheen and color. Oil and oil/varnish blends bring out color in the wood and produce a satin sheen. Wiping varnish also brings out color and is glossy. Shellac or lacquer applied on a lathe could be glossy or satin. Wax, which provides too little protection to be considered seriously as a finish for most objects, has a real place for decorative objects. Wax produces a soft, satin sheen, and most important, leaves the wood very close to its natural color. All other finishes darken the wood and bring out more color.

Floors The most important quality you want for floors is durability. Polyurethane is clearly the best choice. If you don't want the solvent smell lingering in your house, or you don't want the yellowing of polyurethane, use a water-based finish. All other finishes will wear very poorly unless they are waxed frequently.

Occasional tables vary in the degree of protection they need. A coffee table in a family room is likely to see a lot heavier use—and need a tougher finish—than a library table in the living room.

3
APPLYING FINISHES

Key Ingredients

Finishing is a simple craft. Anyone can learn to do it well. The objective is no more complicated than transferring a liquid stain or finish from a can to the wood. There are only three tools to choose from: a rag, a brush, and a spray gun, as shown in the photo. Each is easy to use. Even a spray gun is no more difficult to operate than a router.

There are several key differences between the three tools:

- The cost
- The speed with which each tool is capable of transferring a stain or finish
- The degree to which each tool is capable of producing a level film
- The limitations the weather imposes on the use of a spray gun

The simplicity of finishing should be evident from this photo. There are only three tools used to apply finishes: a rag, a brush, and a spray gun. Compare this selection to the almost countless number of hand and machine-powered tools used for quality woodworking.

Cost

Rags cost very little, or nothing if you make an effort to save old, worn-out cotton clothing. In addition, inexpensive paper towels can often be substituted for rags for small jobs. Brushes are somewhat more expensive. In contrast, even the cheapest spray outfits that are capable of doing basic wood finishing cost $200 or more. So, if cost is a factor, you may be limited to using rags and brushes.

Speed

You can apply a stain or finish to a large area faster with a rag or spray gun than you can with a brush. Rags are best used when you intend to wipe off all the excess, as is usually the case with stains and oil finishes. Spray guns are effective for applying any stain or finish, whether you plan on wiping off the excess or leaving it to build a film.

In comparison, brushes are inefficient tools, because they can carry only a small amount of the liquid stain or finish at a time. You have to constantly dip the brush back into the liquid to reload it. On the other hand, there is no waste with a brush as there is with a spray gun.

Also associated with speed is the ease of clean up. Rags and sponge brushes can simply be thrown away. Quality bristle brushes and spray equipment require time to clean after use.

Film Leveling

In cases where you are not wiping off the excess, leveling is very important. While you can always sand the finish to remove flaws and make it level, this requires extra work, and carries with it the risk of cutting through the finish and causing damage that is difficult to repair. The goal in applying any finish is to get it as level as possible from the start. The three tools differ in their ability to produce a level film.

It is nearly impossible to apply a stain or finish with a rag without leaving deep ridges in the film. The exception is when you use the technique of French polishing, which can only be done with shellac. (The product sold as "padding lacquer" is actually shellac.)

Brushes perform better than rags, but they leave brush marks. This is true even with sponge brushes, which leave ridges at the edges of each brush stroke.

Spray guns produce the most level surface of the three tools. But even the best spray guns leave a light pimply texture called "orange peel."

So, it is not possible to apply a perfect finish using any tool unless you wipe off all the excess after each coat. All three tools leave flaws in the finish film. To make a finish perfect, you have to level it using sandpaper and then rub it to the sheen you want, using steel wool or rubbing compounds, as shown in the photo. It usually is considerably easier to sand a sprayed finish level than a brushed finish. And a brushed finish, in turn, is easier to sand level than a rag-applied finish.

Weather

If you live in a cold climate and can't apply finishes outdoors for a large part of the year, you will have problems using a spray gun. Spray guns create a lot of overspray which will float around the room and land on everything including your work unless you exhaust it. Exhausting overspray presents two problems: replacing the exhausted air with warm air, and trapping the overspray before it gets to the fan and builds up causing a fire hazard.

Not only is overspray a mess, it is also a waste of material. In contrast, rags and brushes transfer all the liquid efficiently from the can to the wood. The only leftover material is evaporating solvent as the coating cures.

Replacing exhausted air with warm air on cold days can be a strain on your heating system. And it can be hazardous to place a heater in the room where you are spraying, especially if there is an open flame in the heater. You risk causing an explosion by spraying in a room where there is an open flame.

To trap overspray, arrange a bank of filters between you and the exhaust fan. Don't allow finish or paint to build up on the fan. In addition, don't allow solvents from a solvent-based paint or finish to be drawn across a motor that is not explosion proof. Though spray guns are easy to use and they produce good results, most hobbyists rely on rags and brushes because of these problems.

No matter how unevenly the finish has been applied, you can always make it nearly perfect by sanding it level and rubbing it, though it may require some work. Here, I just poured the finish onto the wood and spread it around with my hand.

Brushes

There are four basic types of brushes: natural bristle, synthetic bristle, sponge, and paint pads, as shown in the photo. Each can be used to transfer stain or finish from the can to the wood. Bristle brushes are the most common and are put together, as shown in *Parts of a Brush*.

Natural-Bristle Brushes

Natural-bristle brushes are made from animal hair. They are the best brushes for use with all stains and finishes except those that contain water. Water softens natural bristles just as it softens human hair, causing the bristles to lose their stiffness and their shape.

The best commonly available natural-bristle brushes are made from Chinese-hog hairs. These hairs are thick enough to provide good stiffness, but the key to their quality is their split ends. It is the thinness of these ends in contact with the surface that determines how smooth and level a stain or finish can be applied. Though China bristle brushes are a little more expensive, the improved results are usually worth it.

Superior even to China bristle in producing a level surface is an ox-hair brush, for use with varnish, or a badger brush, for either varnish or shellac, as shown in the photo on the opposite page. Ox hair brushes usually combine ox hair and China bristle. Badger brushes usually combine badger and skunk bristle. Both types are difficult to find, but you may be able to order them from your paint dealer. They are two to three times as expensive as good China bristle brushes. If you clean them

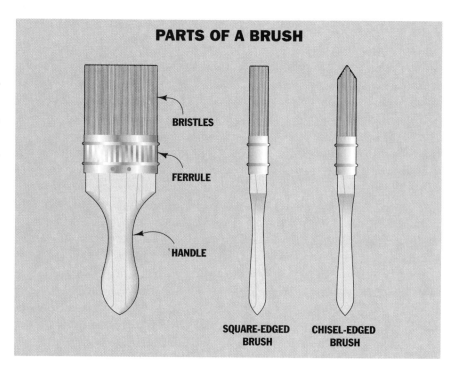

PARTS OF A BRUSH

BRISTLES

FERRULE

HANDLE

SQUARE-EDGED BRUSH

CHISEL-EDGED BRUSH

well after each use, they will last a long time, so the additional cost per use will be minimal.

Synthetic-Bristle Brushes

Synthetic-bristle brushes are made from polyester and nylon. These brushes became popular for use with latex paint, because natural bristles lose their shape in water. The better synthetic-bristle brushes also have split ends and perform almost as well as natural-bristle brushes. Synthetic-bristle brushes are the best choice for all water-based products and work fairly well with oil-based finishes, too.

Of the common types of brushes, the most popular and versatile are those with bristles, whether the bristles are natural or synthetic. Sponge brushes are popular because they are cheap; most people throw them away after each use. Pad applicators are limited to use on flat surfaces; they are excellent for floors.

Sponge Brushes

Sponge brushes are cheap and are usually considered throw-away items. They are very effective for use with all finishing products except lacquer, which dissolves them. Some sponge brushes can also be dissolved by the alcohol in shellac after a period of time. Sponge brushes deposit a very level film, but they leave ridges at the edges of each brush stroke which are usually quite pronounced.

Paint Pads

Paint pads are flat sponge material to which many tiny fibers are attached. The pads are usually held in a plastic handle. Paint pads are effective for applying all finishing products, except lacquer and sometimes shellac, to a flat surface. They attain their ultimate usefulness in floor finishing.

The brushes that lay down the most-level film are those with ox hair and badger hair bristles. Ox hair (left) works well with varnish. Badger hair (right) works well with both varnish and shellac.

RIPPINGS

HOW TO KNOW A GOOD BRUSH

The best brushes have bristles that are "flagged," or split into several strands. To tell if a brush has split ends, spread the bristles until you can separate one from the group. Hold this bristle between two fingers and push down on its end. If the brush is China bristle or a good-quality synthetic bristle, the end should split into two or more strands. Finishing with a flagged brush is faster than with a nonflagged brush since the bristles can carry more finish. And because there are more bristles in contact with the surface, a flagged brush leaves a smoother coat.

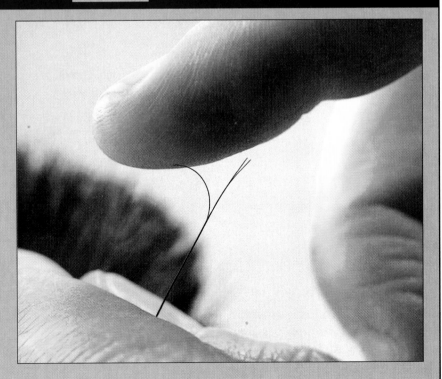

Caring for Brushes

If you use a good-quality brush, you will want to clean it and wrap it up after each use. It is wise, in fact, to clean it before you use it the first time in order to remove any loose bristles or dirt.

I believe that the step of cleaning brushes (or not cleaning them) is more psychological than it is physical. Woodworkers and homeowners often don't clean their brushes well because they consider the job done when the brushing is done—cleaning up afterward is a nuisance at best. You will find that you will enjoy finishing more if you make brush cleaning an important part of the finishing process. It's much the same as what happens when you spend some time getting a chisel or hand plane tuned and sharp. You then enjoy using the tool more because you have invested some time in it. It also helps if you understand how to clean a brush effectively.

The goal in cleaning a brush is to get it to the point that the soap will make suds easily. This is the indication that the brush is clean.

Cleaning Steps

The procedure for cleaning brushes varies a little depending on the finish you are using. In all cases, however, the last step is to wash the brush in soap and water, and store it in the cardboard holder it came in, or in a wrapping of heavy paper like that from a supermarket bag, as shown in the photo. The purpose of wrapping is to make sure the bristles dry straight. You can use any mild soap. A convenient one is dishwater soap. The idea is to wash the brush until it is clean enough that the soap makes suds.

Variations in the cleaning procedure occur in the steps leading up to the soap-and-water washing, and depend on the stain or finish you are using. For example, the only prior step required when using water-based stains and finishes is to rinse the brush in water, then wash with mild soap and water. To clean a brush used for shellac and lacquer, rinse it first in alcohol (for shellac) or lacquer thinner (for lacquer), or in a solution of half-and-half household ammonia and water. Again, finish by washing with a mild soap.

Cleaning Up after Oil-Based Finish

The most difficult brushes to clean are those used for oil-based stains and finishes. These include any stain or finish that thins with paint thinner (mineral spirits). The main reason brushes used in these products are difficult to clean is the paint thinner itself. It is difficult to get the soap to make suds when there is paint thinner in the brush.

STEP 1 Begin cleaning by rinsing the brush once or twice in paint

After cleaning a brush, always store it in its original cardboard container (bottom) or wrap it in heavy construction paper or paper from a brown bag (top). This keeps the bristles straight and keeps dirt from getting in the brush.

thinner. Squeeze the bristles against the bottom of a container (jar or coffee can) that contains an inch or two of paint thinner, or wring out the bristles several times after running your fingers through them. Wear gloves when doing this to keep your skin from drying out or having an allergic reaction.

STEP 2 Change the paint thinner frequently, as it becomes

RIPPINGS

RECLAIMING BRUSHES

If you allow paint or finish to harden on a brush, you can often reclaim the brush by letting it soak in the solvent for the finish (this works with shellac and lacquer), or in paint stripper (this sometimes works for water-based and oil-based coatings). Next, scrub the bristles, with a wire brush if necessary, to knock off as much of the softened finish as possible. Finish by washing the brush in soap and water.

You can store a brush for a day or two without cleaning it by hanging it in a container of thinner. Slide a small dowel through the hole in the brush handle and rest the dowel on the top of the container. If the container isn't deep enough, drill a hole farther down the handle. The solvent should come nearly up to the top of the bristles. Place a plastic coffee-can lid with a cutout for the brush over the jar to keep the solvent from evaporating.

saturated with stain or finish, and keep washing the brush until you feel it is clean. You may want to keep three or four covered coffee cans set up specifically for brush cleaning. Label the cans "First Rinse," "Second Rinse," et cetera. Then you can cycle your brushes through from one can to the next. As the thinner in each can gets dirty, you can pour it into the previous rinse, thus recycling your thinner. When the thinner in the first can is too dirty to use, let it sit for a while. Eventually the solids will settle to the bottom and you can pour off the thinner to reuse.

STEP 3 The final step before washing with soap and water is to rinse the brush in lacquer thinner. This is the trick. Lacquer thinner removes the oiliness left by the paint thinner so that the soap succeeds in making suds after only one or two washings. Without the lacquer thinner rinse, you will have the frustration of washing many more times in soap and water. You could substitute lacquer thinner for the earlier paint-thinner washes, of course, but lacquer thinner is more toxic and more expensive.

If you think you may want to use the brush again within a day or two, and you'd rather not go to the trouble of cleaning it, you can store it in a can or jar containing the solvent or thinner for the finish you are using. Alcohol is the solvent for shellac. Lacquer thinner is the solvent for lacquer. Water is the thinner for water-based stains and finishes. And paint thinner (mineral spirits) is the thinner for oil stains, varnish, and polyurethane. Hang the brush in the container of liquid so that the liquid comes almost to the top of the bristles, as shown in the photo. Don't let the brush rest on the bottom of the container or it will assume a permanent bent shape.

SOLVENT DISPOSAL

If you use a brush with varnish or solvent-based polyurethane, there is no way to avoid using solvents to clean it. How do you dispose of these solvents? It is illegal and unwise to throw them on the ground, because they could soak down into the ground water. It is also illegal, and very messy, to pour solvents down a drain.

The best solution is to reuse the solvent. If you store used solvent in a container, all the solids will settle to the bottom. You can then decant the solvent and reuse it for cleaning, at least for the first couple of rinsings. Continue this recycling, and you will also save a little money.

But eventually it will be time to get rid of this well-used solvent. If your town doesn't have a system for disposing of solvents, the best solution is to let it evaporate into the atmosphere. Place the solvent in a container in a secure area (not where children or animals can get to it, and not in the vicinity of any flame or spark), and let it evaporate. A faster way is to spray the solvent into the air through a spray gun or spread it thin on a concrete driveway. In some areas this may be illegal; check your local codes.

Spray Guns

Spray guns have been in use for about a hundred years. They are used extensively in factories and shops that do woodworking and refinishing because they rapidly transfer a liquid stain or finish to create a near level film on the wood surface.

Spray guns work by breaking up, or "atomizing," a liquid into a fine mist. Any liquid stain or finish can be sprayed through a spray gun. Though the results are more level than those that a brush or rag can accomplish, the stain or finish retains its inherent characteristics. Varnish, for example, still cures slowly, so dust is a problem. Water-based products still raise the grain of wood, and shellac still cures slowly to a soft film if it is old.

Conventional and HVLP Spray Guns

There are two kinds of spray guns (shown in the photo) used

There are two air sources for spray guns: compressors (top) and turbines (bottom). Compressors can be used to power either conventional or HVLP (conversion) spray guns. Turbines power only HVLP spray guns.

for wood finishing. They are classified as either conventional (high pressure) or high-volume, low-pressure (HVLP), but their basic configuration is the same, as shown in *Spray Gun Anatomy.*

Conventional spray guns are powered by compressed air, usually between 25 and 50 pounds per square inch (psi), which means you need to own a compressor to use one. The compressed air enters the gun through a fitting in the handle and exits through an air nozzle at the front of the gun. If the gun is fitted with a cup to hold the liquid stain or finish, the compressed air creates a partial vacuum which draws up the liquid. If the liquid is held in a separate tank, the tank is pressurized to deliver the liquid through the gun. High-pressure streams of air cross the liquid stream as it exits the gun, atomizing it in a fan-shaped or circular pattern.

HVLP spray guns operate in the same manner, except that they use a high volume of air instead of pressure to atomize the liquid. Because there is too little pressure to create a vacuum, the cup holding the liquid is pressurized. This pushes the liquid out of the nozzle. The liquid is then

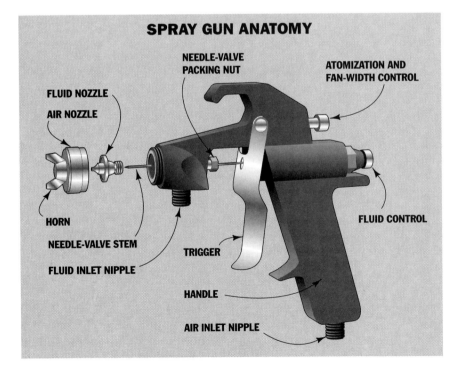

SPRAY GUN ANATOMY

FLUID NOZZLE

AIR NOZZLE

NEEDLE-VALVE PACKING NUT

ATOMIZATION AND FAN-WIDTH CONTROL

HORN

NEEDLE-VALVE STEM

FLUID INLET NIPPLE

TRIGGER

FLUID CONTROL

HANDLE

AIR INLET NIPPLE

SHOP SOLUTIONS: A Temporary Spray Setup

A simple hobby spray booth can be constructed by placing a bank of furnace filters in front of a window fan. The filters will catch the particles of stain and finish in the overspray. However, they won't catch solvent. So if you're spraying anything other than water-based stains and finishes, you should use a fan with an explosion-proof motor mounted away from the blade. Such fans are available through industrial suppliers and some stores that cater to the autobody refinishing trade. Plastic sheeting can be used to create temporary walls to protect the rest of the room from overspray, as well as holding dust at bay. Change the filters frequently so they don't become clogged with finish. Also, don't allow finish to build up on the fan blades. Clean them periodically if necessary. Add more filters if it seems as though too much finish is getting through.

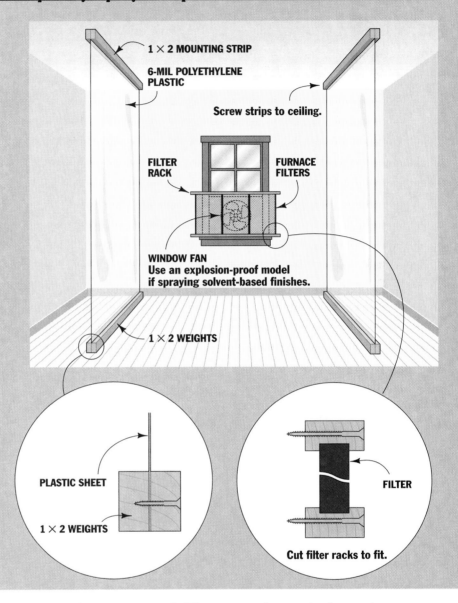

1 × 2 MOUNTING STRIP

6-MIL POLYETHYLENE PLASTIC

Screw strips to ceiling.

FILTER RACK

FURNACE FILTERS

WINDOW FAN
Use an explosion-proof model if spraying solvent-based finishes.

1 × 2 WEIGHTS

PLASTIC SHEET

1 × 2 WEIGHTS

FILTER

Cut filter racks to fit.

atomized and shaped into a fan or circular pattern by the high volume of air coming through the air nozzle. If a separate tank is used to supply the liquid, it has to be pressurized, just as with a conventional gun.

Conventional guns are somewhat faster than HVLP guns, but they also waste a lot of material as overspray—as much as 70 percent in some cases. While they don't apply finish as fast, HVLP guns are much more efficient in transfer-ring finish from can to wood. This will cut down on your material costs, as well as the amount of polluted air you're generating.

With either system, you get what you pay for. The better the quality of the spray gun, the finer the mist, or atomization, it creates. The finer the atomization, the less pronounced the "orange peel," or pimply texture, left on the surface.

If you are considering a new spray setup, look at some of the new "conversion" guns that are coming on the market. These are HVLP guns that run off of compressed air. The older conversion models required a large compressor (at least 5 hp) to generate the necessary volume of air, but some of the newer systems can run off a comparatively small machine ($1\frac{1}{2}$ hp). A conversion gun gives you the benefits of HVLP along with a compressor you can use for other purposes.

Applying Wipe-On Finishes

The easiest way to apply a finish is to wipe it onto the wood, then wipe off most or all of the excess before the finish cures, as shown in the photo. Any finish can be applied this way, but those that cure more slowly are easier because you have more time to complete the process.

The most popular wipe-on finishes are boiled linseed oil, pure tung oil, wiping varnish, and oil/varnish blends. Some finishers apply water-based finishes by wiping, and many woodturners apply shellac or lacquer to their turnings with a rag while the object is still on the lathe. Of course, shellac is often applied to furniture with a cloth using the technique called French polishing. (See "French Polishing" on page 46.)

There are two ways to apply a finish by wiping. You can either soak a rag with the finish and wipe it onto the wood, or pour the finish directly onto the wood and spread it around with a rag.

Whichever method you choose (you could use both together), the

Slow-curing finishes, such as oil, oil/varnish blends, and wiping varnish, are very easy to apply by wiping onto the wood and then wiping off the excess. This easy application technique makes these finishes very popular.

objective is to cover the surface, or a section of the surface, and then remove all or most of the excess before the finish begins to set. If you are wiping off all the excess, it doesn't matter in which direction you apply the finish or remove it. But if you are leaving some of the excess, you should remove the fin-

ish by wiping in the direction of the wood grain wherever possible. This is to ensure that any signs of wiping strokes that you leave behind are disguised as much as possible by the wood grain. Remember that you should always remove all the excess when using linseed oil, pure tung oil, and oil/varnish-blend finishes because these finishes don't cure hard.

STEP 1 Wipe or pour the finish on the surface and spread it around. With oil, oil/varnish blends, and wiping varnish finishes, it's best to keep the surface wet with finish for five to ten minutes before removing the excess. During this time, apply more finish to any dry places you notice on the wood; these areas are caused by all the finish having soaked into the wood. Keep the surface wet until no more

---

FACT OR FICTION

HAND-RUBBING NONSENSE

Many writers and manufacturers encourage hand rubbing oil, oil/varnish-blend, and wiping-varnish finishes into the wood rather than simply wiping them on and wiping off the excess. The reason given is that rubbing will increase penetration. In fact, no benefit is gained by rubbing (unless you count the abrasive benefit you might get from calloused hands). The depth a finish penetrates into the wood is not increased by rubbing; it is determined primarily by how long the finish stays wet on the surface of the wood. Each of these finishes will penetrate all the way through the wood if it can find a passage and if it is kept wet on the surface long enough.

dry places appear for several minutes. The purpose of this step is to get enough finish into the wood to completely seal it with the first coat.

STEP 2 Allow the first coat of finish to cure. The amount of time this takes will vary depending on the finish and the weather conditions. But the longer the finish cures, the harder it will get—and the easier it will be to sand. Generally, boiled linseed oil, wiping varnish, and oil/varnish blends need to cure overnight. Pure tung oil needs two or three days. Water-based finishes, shellac, and lacquer need only a couple of hours.

STEP 3 The wood surface will always be a little rough after the first coat no matter which finish you use or whether or not you wipe off all the excess. That's because the finish encases raised wood fibers (they are so soft you won't feel them before applying the finish) and locks them in an upright position. Sand this rough surface smooth before applying the next coat of finish, as shown in the photo on page 42. Use sandpaper that is finer than the last grit that you used to sand the wood. The finer the sandpaper grit you use at this point, the smoother you will make the surface feel.

STEP 4 When you have made the surface smooth to the touch, clean off the dust and apply a second coat. If you are leaving a little excess with each coat, continue applying coats until you have the buildup that you want. Remember that you can always sand out flaws, such as dust or streaks left by the rag, and apply another coat.

If you are removing all the excess finish, as you must with linseed oil, pure tung oil, and oil/varnish blends, you can usually do so immediately after application. The first coat should have sealed the wood, so no dry places will occur because the finish can no longer soak into the wood. Wipe off the excess finish from this coat, and in most cases you are done. You can try a third coat, but if it doesn't improve the sheen, it has done no good.

WHAT TO DO WITH OILY RAGS

Many finishes that are commonly wiped onto wood contain linseed oil or tung oil. Both of these oils are capable of spontaneous combustion if soaked rags are not properly disposed of. Linseed oil, both raw and boiled, is more dangerous than tung oil, but tung oil will spontaneously combust if the conditions are right.

There are two ways to dispose of oily rags safely. Either expose the rags to air so the heat that is generated by the curing reaction can dissipate, or keep the rags from contact with oxygen so no curing occurs and no heat is generated.

To permit the heat to dissipate, hang rags over the edge of a trash can, table, tree limb, or fence, as shown in the photo; or lay them out on the floor. There is no possibility of fire as long as fresh air can get to all parts of the rags. Make it a habit to drape oily rags over the edge of a trash can or table immediately after using them, even if you intend to take them outside later; something may distract you, causing you to forget. Once the oil in the rag has cured, the rag will become stiff and you can safely throw it in the trash. A rag containing cured oil is no different in terms of hazardous waste than a piece of wood that has had an oil finish applied to it.

To prevent oxygen from allowing the curing process to take place, put oily rags in water or in an airtight container. This is an effective way to prevent spontaneous combustion. What many safety instructions fail to mention is that the rags can still spontaneously combust when you take them out of the water or airtight container. So you should still spread the rags out before throwing them away.

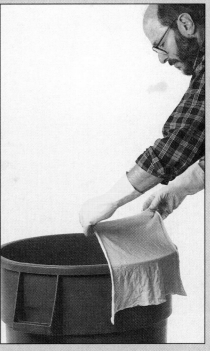

By allowing air to get to all parts of an oily rag, you ensure that heat generated by the curing process won't cause the rag to combust.

PUSHING THE LIMITS: Wet Sanding

With many wipe-on finishes, you can often combine two steps—sanding between coats and applying additional coats—as long as you remove all the excess finish. Each time you apply a new coat of finish, instead of wiping off the excess right away, sand the surface with very fine (400-or 600-grit) sandpaper. Use the finish as a lubricant for the sandpaper. This technique works best, of course, with very slow-curing oil and oil/varnish-blend finishes. Wiping varnish usually cures too fast. The benefit of wet sanding is that you can sand relatively little and still create a surface equal in feel and appearance to one that has been sanded to this fine a grit before applying the finish. Note that wet sanding works only if you then remove all the excess finish. Otherwise, you will leave dust in the film.

Maintaining a Wiped-on Finish

Because wiped-on finishes are almost always very thin, they wear quickly and require periodic maintenance to look and perform their best. The best way to maintain a thin, wiped-on finish is to recoat it now and then as it begins to look a little dry or show wear. Recoating can be done with the same finish you used initially, or with any other wipe-on finish.

You can also maintain a wiped-on finish with paste wax because it will reduce wear. Apply the paste wax as you would to any other finish. See "Caring for Furniture" on page 86 for further details on applying wax.

Woodworkers often choose a wiped-on finish for its ease of application and its easy repairability. They are right on both counts; most wiped-on finishes go on easily and are easy to repair. But there is more to the repair issue. Repairing a thin wiped-on finish is often successful because of its thinness. Any finish, if thin enough, can be repaired easily no matter how it was applied. Just apply another coat of finish. The new coat of finish will disguise any superficial scratches and help them blend with the rest of the surface.

After the first coat of a wiped-on finish dries, you'll have to sand the surface to make it feel really smooth. You can use sandpaper, very fine steel wool or Scotch-Brite pads for this step. Sandpaper cuts better and faster, but the other two are better for getting into recesses.

TROUBLESHOOTING

HOW TO HANDLE BLEEDING
A short time after you wipe off the first coat of an oil or oil/varnish-blend finish, you may notice small drops of finish reappearing on the wood. This is called "bleeding" or "bleedback." It is usually caused by the thinner in the finish drawing the finish back out of the pores as it evaporates. Or a temperature difference could be making the finish expand out of the pores. Whatever the cause, you should continue wiping off any bleeding every half hour or so until it stops. This may require that you apply the finish early in the day.

Brushing a Finish

Brushing a clear finish is no more complicated than brushing paint. You'll quickly get the hang of how to hold the brush and how fast to move it. The feel of the product tells you almost immediately how long you have to brush and rebrush an area. Fast-curing coatings, such as shellac, lacquer, and water-based finishes, become tacky quickly. Slow-curing coatings, such as varnish and polyurethane, allow more time.

Cleanliness

The main difference between brushing finishes and brushing paint is cleanliness. Keeping everything clean is more important when applying clear finishes because dust and dirt show up more than they do in paint. As much as possible, try to follow these cleanliness rules when brushing a clear finish:

- Transfer the amount of finish you expect to use for a job from the original container to a clean glass, metal, or plastic container. This way, you won't contaminate your entire supply with the dust you will probably pick up on your brush.
- If you suspect that there might be dirt or solidified finish in the original container, strain the finish through a paint strainer (available from paint stores) or clean cheesecloth as you are transferring it, as shown in the photo.
- Be sure your brush is clean. A new brush should be washed in soap and water before using. Then, if you want to use the brush immediately with varnish,

A freshly opened can of finish is usually clean and doesn't need to be strained. But dirt or pieces of cured finish will almost always have fallen into previously opened cans, so it is wise to strain the finish before using. The easiest way is to pour it through a paint strainer into another clean container.

RIPPINGS

FOR LEVEL RESULTS, THIN THE FINISH

The thinner a finish, the easier it is to brush level. This is true for all finishes. If you are having problems with brush marking, try thinning the finish with the appropriate thinner (paint thinner for varnish and polyurethane, alcohol for shellac, lacquer thinner for lacquer, water or a proprietary solvent supplied by the manufacturer for water-based finish). You can thin any finish except water-base as much as you want. The only drawback is that the coat will be thinner. Adding a lot of water to water-based finishes may raise the surface tension of the finish so much that it beads on the wood instead of flowing out.

polyurethane, shellac, or lacquer, rinse it in lacquer thinner.

- Remove dust from the wood before beginning. Instead of using a dust brush or compressed air, which will stir up dust that could settle on your work, use a vacuum, tack rag, or water-dampened cloth. A vacuum works with any finish. Sticky tack rags, which you can buy at paint stores, work on all finishes except water-base. With these finishes use only a cloth that has been very lightly dampened with water; a tack rag might leave a sticky residue that would prevent a water-based finish from flowing out level. Just before you begin to brush on the finish, wipe over the surface with your clean hand to pick up any small amount of remaining dust Then remove the dust from your hand by wiping it on a clean cloth or against your pant leg.
- Work in as dust free a room as possible. If you do your finishing and woodworking in the same room, sweep the floor and then let the dust settle for several hours. Just before you begin, dampen the floor around your finishing area so you don't kick up dust walking around. An easy way to do this is with a pump-spray bottle.

Lighting

In addition to keeping everything as clean as possible, you must arrange the lighting on the object you are finishing so that you can always see a reflected light on the surface of the wood. If you don't have a reflection, you might as well be blindfolded, (See the photos on page 44). A reflection is especially critical on vertical surfaces, so that you can see the runs and sags when they occur and remove the excess finish until the problem stops.

Brushing

If you are brushing water-based finish, shellac, or brushing lacquer, each of which dries rapidly, move fast enough so that each new brush stroke overlaps a stroke that is still wet. This is called "keeping a wet edge." It is important because if the previous stroke has begun to set up, your brush will drag it, resulting in ridges curing in the finish. If ridges do occur, quickly wash off the finish with the appropriate thinner or solvent and begin again. Or, let the finish cure, then sand the surface until it is level, and apply another coat.

All finishes are sensitive to the weather, but water-based finishes are especially so. They are also difficult to brush without serious bubbling problems. Try to work in conditions

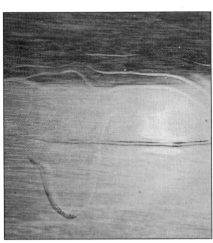

It can't be overemphasized how important it is to arrange lighting so that you can see a reflection on your work as you apply the finish. You can't see what is happening without a reflection. In the left photo the surface looks smooth. But in the right photo, a reflection reveals that the finish is running and sagging.

as close as possible to 70°F and 40 percent humidity. Don't overbrush the finish, or you risk raising more bubbles. The best procedure is to try to lay down a level coat that you don't have to go back over, but this is difficult. It also helps to keep the

coats as thin as possible, so that bubbles pop out and disappear, but this is also difficult. If all else fails, change

It's almost impossible to brush a finish perfectly level, with the brush strokes lined up just right, on the first pass. Therefore, it's usually wise to go back over the finish and tip it off before it begins setting up. Tipping off levels the finish and lines up brush strokes. You have less time to tip off with fast-drying finishes like shellac, lacquer, and water-based finish than with varnish and polyurethane.

TROUBLESHOOTING

SLOW CURING

All finishes cure more slowly in low temperatures and high humidities. The impact of weather conditions on curing is probably the single most overlooked factor in achieving good finishing results. You apply a coat of polyurethane one day and everything goes well. The next day the second coat won't harden. It stays tacky on the surface for days. You used exactly the same can of finish and did everything exactly the same way. So what went wrong? The weather changed. Try to keep the room in which you are working as close as possible to 70° F and 40 percent humidity.

The wood itself can also cause oil and varnish finishes to cure more slowly. So-called oily woods, especially exotic species like teak, rosewood, and cocobolo, contain oil-like resins that are drawn up into the finish when you wipe or brush it onto the wood. By acting like paint thinner that doesn't evaporate, the resins slow the curing of the finish, sometimes very significantly. To keep resins from causing trouble, you should wipe them off the surface of the wood just before you apply the finish. Use a fast-evaporating solvent like naphtha or lacquer thinner. Apply the finish soon after this solvent evaporates, or the resins will have time to come back up to the surface.

TROUBLESHOOTING

PREVENTING PROBLEMS WHEN BRUSHING A FINISH

There are a number of problems that can occur as you're brushing that are easy to prevent or correct.

Runs and Sags To remove runs and sags before they cure, drag your brush over a clean jar edge to remove excess finish. Then rebrush the finish, as shown in the photo below, while continuing to remove the excess from the brush. Apply finish and remove runs and sags a section at a time, so that they don't have time to harden.

Brush Marks and Air Bubbles To lessen brush marks and air bubbles curing in the finish, add a little more of the appropriate thinner to the finish. The added thinner gives the finish more time to flatten out. It also gives bubbles more time to pop out and allows the finish to flow back level. Bubbles are caused by turbulence created by your brush, as shown in the photo below, whether or not you shake or stir the finish. You can't avoid bubbles. The trick is to get them to pop out before the finish skins over and traps them.

Dust There is no way to totally eliminate dust settling on your finish. If the dust nibs are worse than you can tolerate, as shown in the photo below, you will need to sand them out. Sand between coats with 220- or finer-grit sandpaper (gray, lubricated sandpaper works best), and after the last coat sand with 600-grit wet-or-dry sandpaper. You can use water, paint thinner, or mineral oil as a lubricant with wet-or-dry sandpaper. Then rub the surface with #0000 steel wool or a rubbing compound to produce an even satin sheen.

After dragging the brush over the edge of the jar to remove excess finish from the bristles, go back over the surface to pick up any extra finish which may cause runs and sags.

Adding thinner reduces brush marks and allows the bubbles time to pop out.

If the finish has been marred by dust, you'll have to sand the surface smooth.

to another brand of water-based finish. The biggest difference between brands is their relative propensity for bubbling. Most do well when the conditions are good. But some are better than others when the conditions aren't ideal.

For slower-drying finishes like varnish and polyurethane, you can

be more relaxed. Begin spreading the finish onto the wood in any direction. As you move from section to section, or across a large surface, "tip off," or lightly brush the varnish in the direction of the wood grain without applying more finish, as shown in the photo on the opposite page. To tip off, hold the brush almost

vertically and use a gentle touch. The purpose is to line up the brush strokes with the wood grain so they are less noticeable. On horizontal surfaces, begin at the far edge and brush from side to side, working toward you so that dust doesn't fall off your arm onto the varnish you've just applied.

French Polishing

French polishing is a method of applying shellac with a cloth so that there are almost no visible application marks (ridges) in the film, as shown in the photo.

You can French polish stained or unstained wood directly, or you can apply a few coats of shellac with a brush or spray gun, sand the surface level, and finish it off by French polishing. Either way you will create a near-perfect finish without having to do anything further to the final coat.

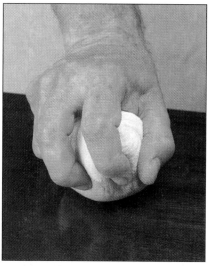

French polishing was often used on high-quality furniture in the nineteenth century before the availability of spray guns, sandpaper, and rubbing compounds. It still produces a finish with a beautiful sheen.

The Technique

STEP 1 Pour enough one-pound-cut shellac onto the French polishing pad so that a little liquid squeezes out when you push your thumb hard into it. Tap the pad against the palm of your hand to disperse the shellac.

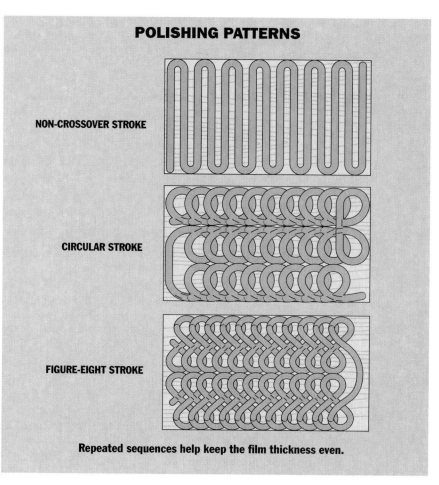

POLISHING PATTERNS

NON-CROSSOVER STROKE

CIRCULAR STROKE

FIGURE-EIGHT STROKE

Repeated sequences help keep the film thickness even.

STEP 2 Begin applying the shellac to the wood by wiping the pad over the wood. No pressure is needed in the beginning. The best way to apply the first couple of coats is in long, straight strokes, working with the grain or in a non-crossover, snakelike pattern, like that shown in *Polishing Patterns*. Don't overlap the strokes any more than necessary.

STEP 3 Continue to apply the shellac in this method, replenishing the pad when necessary. When the pad begins dragging because it is sticking to the shellac already deposited, place a drop or two of a light oil, such as mineral oil, onto the bottom of the pad and disperse it by tapping the pad against your hand. Change your rubbing pattern to circles and figure eights, as shown, to aid in depositing an even coat over

the entire surface, and begin applying a little pressure.

STEP 4 You should pay special attention to the edges because they tend to be neglected, while the mid-

RIPPINGS

SIZE THE PAD TO THE JOB

The most common problem people have when French polishing is getting the surface too soft and damaging it with the pad. The remedy is to use a smaller pad on small surfaces (so you don't pad over the same places so quickly), and to move the pad slowly. If you can feel a tackiness when you touch the surface with your hand, the finish is too soft. Stop and let it harden.

dle gets a thick buildup. Move the pad slowly, about the speed you would move a brush when painting. Add more shellac to the pad, followed by a drop or two of oil, whenever the pad gets dry.

Work with a reflected light on the surface. Once you begin adding oil to the pad, you should notice a "comet tail" following the pad. This is the alcohol evaporating, and it is an indication that everything is going well. The shellac and alcohol are being deposited onto the surface through the oil, which acts as a cushion to keep the pad from sticking to the surface. The alcohol evaporates, leaving a thin layer of shellac.

Be careful not to work the surface so much that it softens and the pad damages it. If this does happen, stop and let the surface cure hard. Store your pad in an airtight jar so you don't have to make a new one

each session. At any point, if the surface becomes ridged or dirty, or your pad leaves a mark, stop and sand the surface lightly with 320-grit or finer sandpaper to remove the flaws. Then continue applying more shellac.

Removing the Oil

Build the finish until you have an even gloss over the entire surface. You won't know for sure that it is even until you remove the oil that you left on the surface with your pad. The oil performs the same function as furniture polish or paste wax. It disguises flaws in the finish. To remove the oil easily, wipe the surface with paint thinner or naphtha. Naphtha evaporates much faster than paint thinner, so you will see the results almost immediately. If you use paint thinner, you will have to wait several minutes until it evaporates.

TROUBLESHOOTING

WHEN FRENCH POLISHING GOES WRONG
You can't ruin a project by French polishing it. Problems can always be fixed. Here are a few alternatives.
- Sand out flaws and apply more finish.
- Remove excess oil on the surface by wiping with paint thinner or naphtha.
- Completely remove what you've done with denatured alcohol or paint stripper and start over.

If there are flaws in the surface, sand lightly and continue applying more shellac. If the surface has an even sheen, you can stop. You may want to apply furniture polish or paste wax to reduce scratching and add a little more life to the finish.

STEP-BY-STEP: MAKING A FRENCH-POLISHING PAD

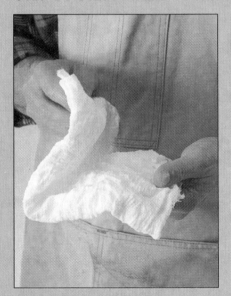

STEP 1 Take a piece of white cheesecloth, cotton cloth, or wool that will fit comfortably into your hand when folded up. Fold the cloth so that the bottom side is smooth.

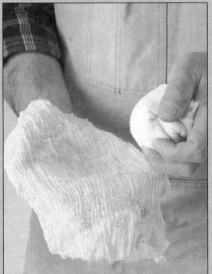

STEP 2 Cover the first wad of fabric with a lint-free cloth, such as tight-woven cheesecloth or a well-washed handkerchief that doesn't stretch.

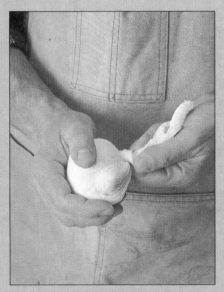

STEP 3 Wrap the second cloth around the first, and twist it tight. The idea is to keep the bottom of the pad smooth and wrinkle-free.

Spraying Finishes

Spraying is messier and more wasteful than applying a finish with a rag or brush. But it's fast, and you get the most level surface possible with any finish-application tool. The slight orange-peel pattern left by a spray gun is far less noticeable than brush marks left by brushes and ridges left by rags.

The physical act of spraying a stain or finish is very simple. Assuming the gun is clean and in good operating condition, and assuming that it and the air source are set properly, all you do is pull the trigger and keep the gun moving perpendicularly to the wood surface. A little hand-eye coordination is required, but not any more than is required to operate a router.

The first couple of times you try to spray, you will probably feel a little out of control, just as you did when you first turned on a router. You will also probably stop the spray gun without releasing the trigger while the gun is still pointing at the wood, causing a buildup of finish. This is equivalent to the time or two a router ran away on you because you should have been pulling or pushing in the opposite direction.

After you've used a spray gun a couple of times, you will have the coordination required to release the trigger when you stop moving the spray gun. Then you will be able to concentrate on technique and settings.

Practice

To get to this point without creating a mess on your project, practice using the spray gun first. Begin by spraying water. Spray it on an outside wall, concrete floor, or scrap plywood. Get a feel for how the gun handles without wasting finish. Then, put finish into the gun and spray it on cardboard or scrap plywood. Finishes are thicker than water, so they spray somewhat differently. Practice spraying both vertical and horizontal surfaces. You will learn very quickly by trial and error how to spray successfully. Again, there is not much to it. But to save a little time, keep the following tips in mind:

- Always hold the gun perpendicularly to the object, as shown in *Proper Spraying*. Don't tilt it vertically, or swing it in an arc horizontally. Any motion away from perpendicular will distribute the finish unevenly. It helps if you keep your wrist locked and direct the spray gun from your elbow and shoulder.
- Move the gun at a steady, even pace. If you move it at irregular speeds, the finish will build up unevenly. (With each finish, you'll soon get a feel for how fast to move the gun to avoid sags and runs.)
- At the end of each spraying stroke, release the trigger to the point that only air passes

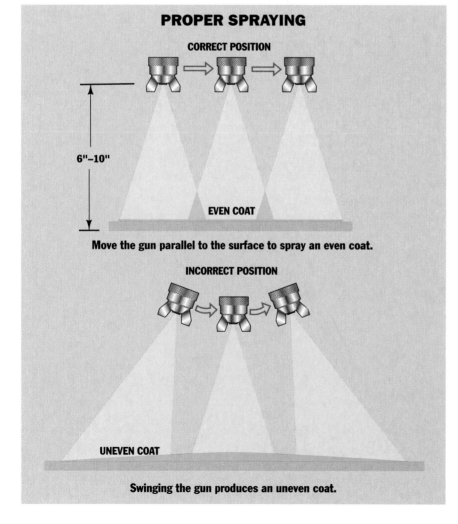

PROPER SPRAYING

CORRECT POSITION

6"–10"

EVEN COAT

Move the gun parallel to the surface to spray an even coat.

INCORRECT POSITION

UNEVEN COAT

Swinging the gun produces an uneven coat.

through the nozzle, or nothing passes through. This reduces waste and overspray, cuts down on finish buildup on the fluid nozzle, and creates less puddling on horizontal surfaces and fewer runs and sags on vertical surfaces. Also, you'll cut down on muscle fatigue since your hand can relax between strokes.

● When spraying an item like a tabletop or cabinet door that has a broad, flat surface, spray the edges before spraying the surface, as shown in *Spraying a Flat Surface.* This will reduce the likelihood of overspray causing roughness on the

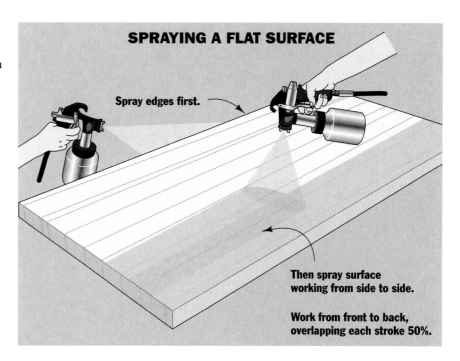

SPRAYING A FLAT SURFACE

Spray edges first.

Then spray surface working from side to side.

Work from front to back, overlapping each stroke 50%.

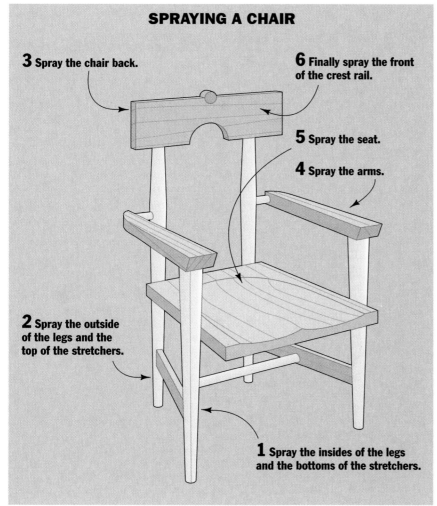

SPRAYING A CHAIR

3 Spray the chair back.

6 Finally spray the front of the crest rail.

5 Spray the seat.

4 Spray the arms.

2 Spray the outside of the legs and the top of the stretchers.

1 Spray the insides of the legs and the bottoms of the stretchers.

surface since any overspray from the edges will be covered when you spray the surface.

● When spraying a large flat surface like a tabletop or cabinet door, overlap each stroke by about 50 percent. This way, as you move across the surface, you will deposit an even thickness.

● When spraying a horizontal surface, begin with the near side and work to the far side so the exhaust doesn't pull overspray onto an already-sprayed area.

● Don't spray directly into inside corners. Spray each side right up to the corner. This will produce the most even buildup with the least overspray.

● Spray the least important parts first and the most important (that is, the most visible) parts last, as shown in *Spraying a Chair.* You want to reduce the possibility of overspray landing on visible parts after they have already been sprayed.

HOW TO ADJUST A SPRAY GUN

To get good results with a spray gun, it must be adjusted properly. The goal is the finest possible atomization and an even spray pattern. Fine atomization, shown in the photo, reduces orange peel. An even spray pattern is necessary to achieve a uniform thickness.

With a compressor-driven gun (either conventional or HVLP), you can improve atomization by increasing air pressure, thinning the finish, or both. With turbine-powered HVLP guns, you can't increase air pressure, so the only way to improve atomization is to thin the finish.

The basic spray pattern should be an elongated oval, as shown in *Spray Patterns.* You can change it to a small circular shape by screwing in the fan-adjustment knob, which is the top screw knob on two-knob spray guns, or by rotating the fan-control template under the air nozzle on one-knob spray guns.

If the spray pattern is half-moon shaped instead of oval, as shown, either a hole in one of the horns on the air nozzle is clogged, or the needle or fluid nozzle is damaged. To find out which, spray some stain, finish, or paint onto a surface, then rotate the air nozzle 180 degrees and spray again. If the half-moon shape changes 180 degrees, a hole is clogged. If it doesn't, either the needle or fluid nozzle is damaged and will have to be replaced.

To set the air pressure in a compressor-powered gun properly, turn the air nozzle so the elongated oval pattern runs horizontally when spraying a vertical surface, as shown in *Setting the*

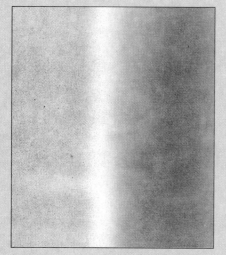

The goal in spraying is to get the finest possible atomization with the spray gun you have. Coarse atomization (left) causes a pimply or orange-peel effect on the surface. Fine atomization produces a more level surface.

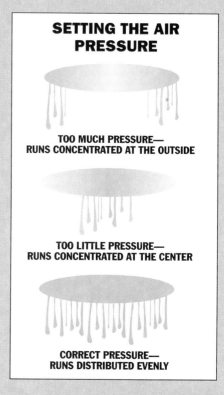

SETTING THE AIR PRESSURE

TOO MUCH PRESSURE— RUNS CONCENTRATED AT THE OUTSIDE

TOO LITTLE PRESSURE— RUNS CONCENTRATED AT THE CENTER

CORRECT PRESSURE— RUNS DISTRIBUTED EVENLY

Air Pressure. Spray a surface until the liquid starts to run. If the pressure is right, the runs will be fairly even across the entire fan width. If the runs are concentrated in the middle, decrease the air pressure in 5-pound increments until the runs are even. If the runs are heaviest on the outsides of the oval and light in the middle, decrease the air pressure in 5-pound increments until the running is even.

SPRAY PATTERNS

INCREASED AIRFLOW

A half-moon pattern indicates a problem.

Typical patterns are symmetrical.

Problem Solving
Fixing a Finish

*There are very few finishing problems that can't be fixed. At the very worst, you can
always resort to a little paint stripper to get a fresh start.*

PROBLEM	SOLUTION
I've applied four coats of tung oil to my oak entertainment center, and even though I sanded the surface smooth after each coat, it still feels rough. What is happening?	Tung oil expands as it absorbs oxygen and cures. The expansion causes the film to lift a little out of the porous grain in the oak, which makes the wood feel rough. You usually have to apply five to seven coats of pure tung oil, sanding between each coat, before the surface stays smooth. Also, it usually takes this many coats to achieve a nice sheen with tung oil.
When I applied a wiping varnish to a cherry chest of drawers, the finish dried before I could get it all wiped off.	If you catch the wiping varnish before it has cured too much, you can usually reliquefy it by applying more wiping varnish or paint thinner. If the wiping varnish has cured beyond reliquefying, you will have to sand the wiping varnish smooth and apply another coat or strip it off with paint stripper and begin again. In the future, work faster or on smaller areas at a time.
The shellac I brushed onto my jewelry box turned milky white. I don't know what happened because I used this same shellac a week before and didn't have any problems.	The weather became more humid, which creates a finishing problem known as "blushing." The rapidly evaporating alcohol solvent cools the surface, which causes moisture in the air to condense on it. The moisture causes the finish to come out of solution, making it appear milky white. The discoloration is usually very superficial and can be easily abraded by rubbing with fine steel wool or a rubbing compound. Alternatively, you can wait until a drier day and then recoat the surface with more shellac. The alcohol solvent will soften the existing blushed shellac, and clear up the color. 
Every time the weather is hot and humid, my lacquer blushes. Is there any way I can spray lacquer on humid days?	In contrast to shellac, there is a way to prevent blushing in lacquer. The trick is to use a slower-evaporating lacquer thinner. This gives the moisture that condenses onto the lacquer more time to evaporate before the lacquer cures. Slower-evaporating lacquer thinner is called "lacquer retarder." You can mix retarder with regular lacquer thinner to get just the right evaporation rate so that blushing is eliminated but curing is not overly slow. There is no commonly available alcohol with which to do the same with shellac.

4
CHOOSING STAINS

Key Ingredients

Staining causes more problems for woodworkers than any other step in finishing. When you apply stain to wood, you may not always get the intended effect. Even worse, because it's often impossible to correct staining problems after they've occurred, you may be stuck with what you have. This frustration causes many woodworkers to shun staining altogether.

This is a shame. If staining is done properly, it enhances the natural beauty of wood much more than simply applying a clear finish, as shown in the photos. Stains intensify the figure and grain of wood to make it appear more alive and interesting. Of course, stains can also be used to change the wood's color.

Before the twentieth century most furniture was left unstained. The high-quality dyes and pigments that we have available today did not exist. Also, the woods that were used, primarily mahogany and walnut, were of very high quality. These woods have since acquired a rich, beautiful patina. Today we use stains both to imitate the patina of aged wood and to make more affordable, but lesser-quality woods more attractive.

During the 1960s and 1970s, styles were influenced by a "back to nature" attitude. As a result, the natural look of wood became very popular. I think that among

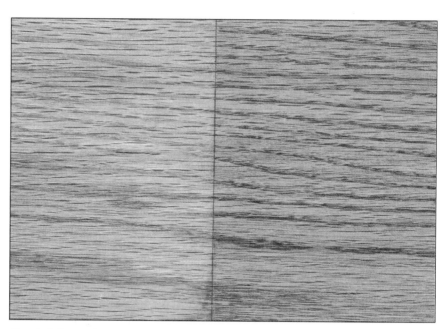

By staining oak, you can call attention to its grain.

A plain and inexpensive wood like poplar can be transformed into a beautiful imitation walnut or mahogany with the application of a stain.

woodworkers, at least, this style was reinforced by the relative ease with which a natural look could be accomplished. All you had to do was apply a couple of coats of oil/varnish blend or wiping varnish finish and wipe off the excess.

We now know that these finishes don't hold up well because they are too thin. Styles have also changed to emphasize an increased range of colors and textures. Even faux (imitation or fake) finishes are back in style.

You may not always choose to color your wood, but it is no longer acceptable not to know how, or to reject staining out of hand. Understanding stains and staining opens up new possibilities for decorating your woodwork.

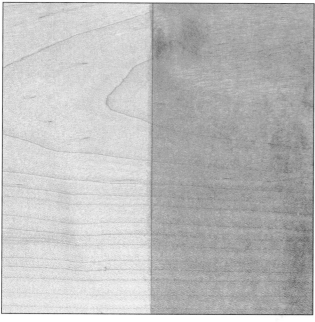

Maple, which is almost white, can be made to look like Early American maple by using a stain.

Light-colored woods like maple can be stained black, or "ebonized," without obscuring the wood's figure.

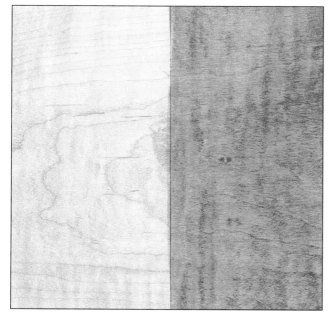

Bird's-eye and curly maple can be given added depth and beauty by applying a stain.

Honduras mahogany has a pinkish color and can be stained to resemble deep reddish brown Cuban mahogany that has aged 200 years.

The Interplay of Wood and Stain

You cannot get predictable results when staining if you don't understand how the wood influences these results. The same stain will produce greatly different effects from one species of wood to another.

Wood is an uneven, porous material composed entirely of soda straw–like channels that carried water and nutrients when the tree was alive, as shown in *A Microscopic View of Wood*. When a tree is milled and the boards are dried of excess water, these channels can absorb stain.

In cases where the strawlike channels run straight and are the same size and evenly spaced, stain is absorbed evenly. But wood is a natural material, and such uniformity rarely exists. The size of the channels often varies, particularly in woods like oak, where there is significant difference in seasonal growth. Swirly areas often exist, and sometimes you'll find pockets of lower or higher density. In addition, ends of the channels may be partially exposed because boards are not always cut exactly along the grain due to the natural taper of the tree.

Any one of these variations will cause stain to color the wood unevenly. You must have an idea of what is likely to occur before you apply a stain, because it's difficult to remove all the stain from wood afterward. It is best to experiment with stain on scrap pieces of the wood you're working with, not only to view the stain color but also to learn the characteristics of the wood before you begin.

Characteristics of Woods

The grain of each wood species will have its influence on how a stain performs, as shown in the photo on the opposite page. More stain is absorbed into the ends of the strawlike channels than into the sides; so end grain and areas where swirly grain angles to the surface will always show up darker, as shown in *How Grain Affects Stain Absorption*. Pine, cherry, birch, and maple are the woods most notorious for having swirly grain. Pine and cherry also often have pockets of lower density that will absorb stain differently than the surrounding wood. Any one of these woods may blotch unattractively when stained.

Coarse-grained woods, such as oak, ash, elm, and chestnut, have different-sized channels and unevenly spaced grain due to a large difference in density between spring- and summer-growth wood. The large channel openings, called pores, in the spring-growth wood retain a lot of stain and become quite dark. The denser, summer-growth wood in between the large pores does not retain much stain, so it is lighter.

Dense, fine-grained woods, such as maple, birch, cherry, poplar, alder, and gum, pose a problem if you want to make them dark. The pores are too small for many stains to color these woods well.

Medium-grained woods, such as walnut, mahogany, and teak, are the easiest to stain evenly because their

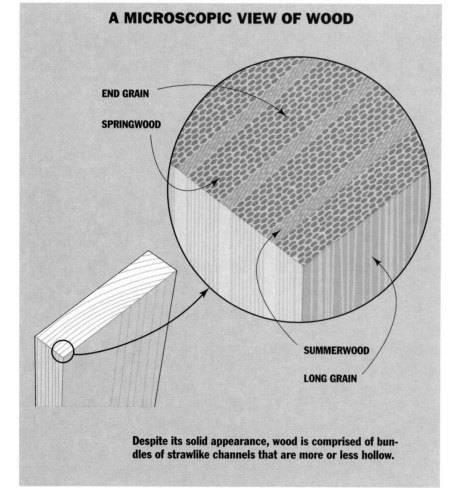

A MICROSCOPIC VIEW OF WOOD

END GRAIN

SPRINGWOOD

SUMMERWOOD

LONG GRAIN

Despite its solid appearance, wood is comprised of bundles of strawlike channels that are more or less hollow.

By applying the same stain to four different woods, you can get four very different looks. Maple has uniform grain that is fairly dense, so the stain doesn't color it deeply. Oak has a very pronounced grain that is highlighted by the stain. Poplar is uniform and less dense than maple, so it stains darker. Mahogany has a reddish tint that affects the stain color.

pores are of fairly uniform size, evenly spaced, and large enough for all stains to be effective. The limited amount of blotching that occurs in these woods is usually considered to be attractive.

Some woods—curly and bird's-eye maple, as well as crotches and burls of various species—have a swirly grain or uneven density that is not only attractive but eagerly sought after. The natural beauty of these woods can be enhanced with stain.

A wood's natural color will also affect the hue you get after staining. For example, walnut is already quite dark, so stain has less effect on it than it would on light woods. Mahogany and cherry have a natural pinkish to reddish coloring, which makes these woods come out redder than you would expect from the color of the stain. The heartwood of poplar is greenish in contrast to the sapwood, which is nearly white, and stained poplar reflects both of these colors.

HOW GRAIN AFFECTS STAIN ABSORPTION

KNOT

SWIRLY GRAIN

END GRAIN

Stain is absorbed most deeply into end grain and swirly grain where the grain angles to the surface.

RIPPINGS

TEST STAINS BEFORE USE
Always keep in mind that the stained wood samples you see in paint stores are only guides to how the stain will look on your wood. Even if the samples are made from the same species you're using, the stain may look different when you get it home. Be sure to test the stain on a scrap of the same wood you will use for your project and to sand to exactly the same grit that you sanded your project to. The more consistent you can be with your test piece, the better the test will show you what to expect. At this point, you don't want surprises.

Types of Stain

When you go to a store and pick out a stain, chances are you are more concerned with the color you want than with other characteristics that will determine how the wood will look and how easy the product will be to apply. These other characteristics are actually more important than the color because you can't change them; it is always possible to change the color of a stain by thinning it or by adding a colored pigment. In fact, some manufacturers supply a neutral base stain material to which you can add pigment to produce any color stain you want.

Other than color, stains vary in three significant ways:
- The type of colorant used: pigment or dye
- The type of binder that is included in the stain to glue the pigment to the wood: oil, varnish, lacquer, or water-based finish
- The thickness of the stain: liquid or gel

Colorant

The colorant in all common stains is either pigment or dye, or a combination of the two. You get very different results depending on which of these colorants is included in the stain, as shown in the photo.

Pigment is natural or synthetically made colored earthen powder. Each pigment particle is large enough to see with your naked eye. These particles are much too big to penetrate into the fibers of wood. Pigment lodges in pores and other cavities, making these areas darker, but it doesn't add as much color to the denser, in-between areas.

Pigment particles also lodge in sanding scratches. The deeper the

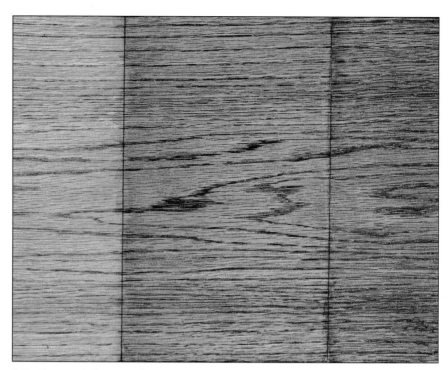

Whether a stain contains pigment, dye, or both as the colorant, makes an important difference in the way the stain looks on wood. On oak, for example, pigment highlights the grain by coloring it more intensely than the dense, in-between parts; dye colors the wood more evenly because it colors all parts well; pigment/dye combinations give results that are somewhere in between.

RIPPINGS

IDENTIFYING A STAIN'S COLORANT

Manufacturers seldom tell you what type of colorant is in their stain. You can find out for yourself by dipping a light-colored wood stirring stick into a can of stain that has been sitting undisturbed on a shelf for several days. Dye doesn't settle like pigment does, so if the liquid near the top of the can colors the stick, the stain contains dye. If there is a lump of solid material collected at the bottom of the can, the stain contains pigment. If there is pigment at the bottom and the stick is colored above as well, the stain contains both dye and pigment.

COMPARING PIGMENT AND DYE

BINDER — PIGMENT PARTICLES — DYE

Pigment lodges in pores and other cavities, making these areas darker. Dye becomes a part of the liquid, so it penetrates everywhere the liquid does and colors the wood more evenly. Dye is capable of coloring wood much darker than pigment without obscuring the wood.

Pigment particles are relatively large and are simply glued to the wood's surface with a binder. Dye, in contrast, totally dissolves in a liquid and penetrates deeply into the wood's fibers.

scratches, the more room the particles have to lodge. So, the coarser the sandpaper you use before staining, the darker the wood will appear, as shown in the photo.

In contrast to pigment, which is insoluble, dye dissolves totally in a liquid. Therefore dye penetrates deeply along with the liquid, into the wood fibers themselves, as shown in

Comparing Pigment and Dye. That is why dyes, unlike pigment, are capable of coloring wood quite dark without obscuring it.

Most stains sold in paint stores and home centers contain either pigment or a combination of pigment and dye. These combination stains are very popular because they produce a richer, darker color than pig-

ment stains on dense woods like maple and a more even coloring on coarse woods like oak. Dye stains are available from mail-order catalogs and speciality woodworking stores.

Binder

Because pigment doesn't penetrate into wood, stains containing pigment require a binder to glue the pigment particles to the wood. Otherwise, the particles could be blown or brushed off the wood after the solvent evaporated. There are four common binders used in stains—oil, varnish, lacquer, and water-based finish.

The binder controls the drying time of the stain—it doesn't affect the way the stain looks. Oil cures the slowest of the four binders. You have more time to apply and wipe off oil-based stains than other stains. You also have to wait longer before applying a finish.

Lacquer cures the fastest of the four binders, so lacquer stains are very useful in production situations. These stains cure fast like lacquer, can be mixed with lacquer, and can be thinned with lacquer thinner.

Varnish and water-based stains cure at a rate in between that of oil and lacquer. Water-based stains have the advantage of containing less petroleum-based (or "organic") solvent than the other stains, but the disadvantage of raising the grain of the wood.

Stains based on oil, varnish, or mixtures of oil and varnish are the easiest to use because they give you plenty of time before drying to remove the excess, and they don't raise the grain. Oil-based stains dry slowly, varnish-based stains, much faster. Most of the stains sold in paint stores and

Because the pigment in pigment stains lodges in irregularities in the wood, it colors coarse-sanded wood darker than fine-sanded wood. Here, the comparison is between maple sanded to 100-grit (right) and sanded to 280-grit (left). It is important that you sand all parts of your project to the same grit before you apply a pigment stain.

home centers are based on oil, varnish, or a combination of the two.

Unfortunately, manufacturers seldom tell you which binder their stain is based on. In the case of water-base and lacquer, it is easy to tell by the solvents or cleanup materials listed on the can. Water-based stains list water as a cleanup material. Lacquer lists lacquer thinner or xylene as a solvent.

Both oil- and varnish-based stains will have petroleum distillate (mineral spirits, paint thinner) listed as an ingredient. To tell what the binder is, pour a little stain onto a nonporous surface, such as glass or the top of the stain can, and let it cure overnight. If the puddle cures soft and wrinkled, the binder is oil or a mixture of oil and varnish. If the puddle cures hard and smooth, the binder is varnish.

Thickness

Some stains are made into a thicker gel form. They can include either pigment or dye as the colorant and any of the four binders, although all gel stains on the market now are varnish-based or water-based.

RIPPINGS

STAIN NAMES ARE ONLY GUIDES
You can't judge the color of a stain by the name. Manufacturers differ in their interpretation of names like fruitwood, colonial American, and mahogany. Always judge a stain by testing how it looks on the type of wood you are staining.

To see the color you will get once a project has been finished, look at the stain while it is still damp—before it dries and lightens. To check for the final color on stain that has already dried, wipe over the stain with a non-interfering liquid. Here, I'm wiping a dry, water-based dye stain with paint thinner to wet the stain without wiping it away.

Liquid stains tend to highlight ugly blotchiness in woods like pine because they penetrate deeper into swirly and less-dense grain. Gel stains don't flow, so they won't penetrate unevenly and won't highlight blotchiness. But neither do gel stains highlight the beautiful grain in woods like bird's-eye maple, while liquid stains do.

Gel stains are like latex wall paint that flows easily when you apply it but stays exactly as the roller leaves it. In the same manner, gel stains are easy to apply, but they don't flow into the wood's pores and fibers like liquid stains do. Thus, gel stains don't accentuate the wood's figure or its flaws as much as liquid stains, as shown in the photo at left. You choose gel stain primarily on the basis of the consistency. The thicker the stain, the less it penetrates, but the more uniformly it will color. This is true whether the colorant used is pigment or dye.

STAINING IN THE REAL WORLD

Color is foremost when considering the choice of a stain. But there are other things to keep in mind to avoid potential problems when planning projects.

Pine Doors and Trim. The problem with pine is blotching. The easiest way to avoid blotching, especially on large surfaces, is to use a gel stain, although you will sacrifice a bit of depth and darkness. Alternatively, you could apply a stain controller before applying the stain. Stain controller is a slow-evaporating, petroleum-based solvent that fills the pores and keeps the stain from penetrating as deeply. Or you can use a toner that is sprayed over a sealed surface. Keep in mind that the stain controller will be difficult to keep even on such a large surface, and a toner won't give any grain definition.

Maple or Birch Dresser. The decision is between a rich, deep color accompanied by possible blotching, on one hand, and a more subdued color with no blotching. A water-soluble dye will produce the most beautiful coloring on these woods, since it penetrates deeply into the wood. But this deep penetration can also lead to a blotchy appearance. You should apply the dye to scrap wood to see if you like the results. If your test piece blotches, chances are the project will, too. For a more even color, you may have to go with a gel stain or a stain controller. Unfortunately, these won't produce a very dark or deep color.

An alternate solution is to spray on light coats of NGR dye. (See "Aniline Dyes" on page 60.) Spray lightly enough so you don't get the wood wet. This will reduce penetration to a minimum. You can make

There are a number of ways that stains are formulated to solve various problems. Get to know how these stains work so that you're ready when the need arises.

the wood as dark as you want without obscuring the grain, and you won't have blotching.

Bird's-Eye or Curly Maple Bench. You don't get the full beauty of these figured woods with a simple finish. Any type of stain, except a gel stain, will make the figure in bird's-eye and curly maple pop. Dye is the most effective. You will probably be happiest with a thinned dye that doesn't make the wood too dark.

An alternative way to color these woods is to apply boiled linseed oil and let it cure for a week before applying the top coats. The linseed oil penetrates deeply into the wood, better highlighting the figure; and because the oil darkens as it ages, the wood comes to approximate the highly valued look of old bird's-eye and curly maple. Any finish can be applied over linseed oil once it has dried thoroughly.

Walnut Coffee Table. Walnut looks good under almost any finish,

without any stain, though you may choose to stain walnut to adjust the wood's color. You may also want to stain walnut to even out any color variations between the dark heartwood and the lighter sapwood.

Mahogany Table. Mahogany usually looks best with a reddish brown dye stain. But pigment stains and pigment/dye combination stains also color mahogany fairly well.

Kitchen Cabinets and Other Large Objects. The problem will be getting an even coloring. Only a stain based on a slow-curing oil binder will allow enough time for you to wipe the excess off easily. All other stains dry too fast, so the surface will have to be divided into smaller sections and stained separately. A lacquer-based stain could be sprayed and either left or wiped off quickly (if wiping, it's best to have two people involved), or an NGR dye stain could be sprayed and left.

Aniline Dyes

Because aniline dyes are important for achieving certain effects and yet are so little understood, they deserve a separate discussion.

Until modern times, wood was seldom dyed, and then only with natural dyes that faded quickly and chemicals that were difficult to use and limited in color choice. Then, beginning in 1859, a range of thousands of dye colors was synthesized from coal tar, and later from petroleum. By the beginning of the twentieth century, these synthetic aniline dyes had completely replaced natural and chemical dyes in the textile and furniture industries.

Each dye color dissolves better in some solvents than in others. As a result, dyes are classified according to the solvent they dissolve in: water, alcohol, or oil. Oil-soluble dyes go by that name even though they are commonly dissolved in paint or lacquer thinners. The name is a throwback to the nineteenth century when neither of those solvents was available and the dyes were actually dissolved in oil.

Each of these dyes is available in powder form that is ready for you to dissolve in the proper solvent, as shown in the photo below. Once a dye is dissolved, it stays in solution. It doesn't settle like pigment. Most suppliers of powder dyes recommend that each ounce of dye be dissolved in 1 quart of solvent for a standard color.

The primary difference between water-, alcohol-, and oil-soluble dyes, besides the solvent, is their resistance to fading. All dyes fade fairly quickly in sunlight compared to pigment, as shown in the photo above. But alcohol-soluble and oil-soluble dyes fade significantly more quickly than water-soluble dyes.

Furniture factories understood the significance of lightfastness and usually chose water-soluble dyes over the others. But water raises the grain of wood, so the factories were forced to wet the wood, let it dry overnight, and then sand off the raised grain before they applied the dye. (See "Grain-Raising Remedies" on page 29.) This slowed their assembly lines.

By the 1930s, petroleum-based solvents became available that would dissolve water-soluble dyes and could be thinned with alcohol or lacquer thinner. These dyes are called non-grain-raising (NGR) dyes, and they are used almost exclusively in the furniture industry and by professional finishers.

Dyes come in powdered form and must be mixed with the appropriate solvent. The standard ratio is 1 ounce of dye to 1 quart of solvent.

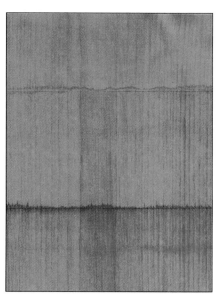

Dyes fade much faster than pigment, especially in sunlight. Here is a board, colored with several brands of dye, which was placed in the sun for one week. The bottom was shielded with tape from the sun.

Today, you can buy NGR dyes that dissolve in alcohol and are even more lightfast than water-soluble dyes.

Using Aniline Dyes

You apply aniline dyes as you would any stain. You can wipe, brush, or spray the dye onto the wood and then wipe off the excess before the dye dries. Or you can wipe, brush, or spray the dye onto the wood and just let it dry.

Besides having the ability to color wood very dark without obscuring the grain, dyes can be lightened or darkened significantly after they have dried on the wood, and they can even be changed to an entirely different color. This is possible because dyes don't contain binders, which are necessary in pigment stains to glue the pigment particles to the wood. Anytime you put the solvent back into contact with a dye, the dye will redissolve.

If the color is too dark, let the solvent evaporate, and then lighten the dye by wiping over with a cloth dampened with more solvent. The solvent puts the dye back into solution, allowing you to remove as much of the color as you want, though you can't remove all the color from the wood, except by sanding.

If the color is too light, wait until the solvent evaporates, then apply another coat of dye and wipe off the excess. The newly applied dye will dissolve the old, making a new solution of double strength and greater darkness. Alternatively, apply another coat of dye and don't remove it all. As the solvent evaporates, the proportion of dye to solvent increases, creating a darker color. You can move back and forth between lighter and darker until you achieve the depth of color you want, as shown in the photo below.

To change red-dyed wood to orange, wipe over with yellow dye. To change red-dyed wood to brown, wipe over with black.

If you want to change the color, apply another color of dye that uses the same solvent as the original, placing it right on top. Then remove the excess. The solvent in the newly applied dye will dissolve the original dye, and the two colors will blend, as shown in the photo above. When you remove the excess dye, the color remaining will be somewhere in between the two colors.

Which Dye to Use?

If you are applying the dye by hand rather than with a spray gun, water-soluble dye is the best choice for most situations. Water-soluble dyes are relatively lightfast and they provide the most working time of all dyes. The solvent (water) is also cheap and nontoxic. The major exception is when you intend to brush a water-based finish over the dye. The water in the finish will redissolve the water-soluble dye and your brush will smear it. In this case, you should use an NGR dye or an oil-soluble dye dissolved in paint thinner to give yourself as much working time as possible. If you are applying dye with a spray gun, and you don't intend to wipe off the excess, an NGR dye will give the best results.

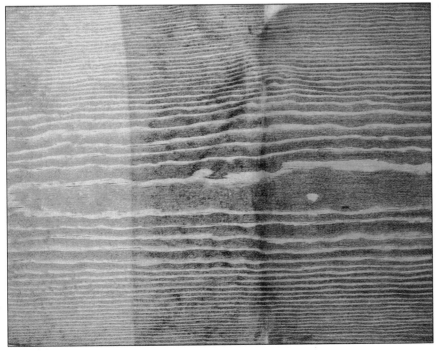

To lighten the color of dyed wood, wash it with the appropriate solvent. To darken it, apply another coat of dye.

5
APPLYING STAINS

Key Ingredients

You can apply stains using any of three tools—rag, brush, or spray gun. You can also pour the stain onto the wood and spread it around, or you can dip the wood into the stain. The method you choose is governed by the tools you have at your disposal and how you want the wood to look.

But regardless of what tools you use, there are really just two ways to apply stain:

● Apply and wipe off all or most of the excess.
● Apply and leave the excess.

Wiping Off the Excess

The most common method of staining is to apply the stain and then remove the excess, as shown in the photo. It makes no difference in which direction you apply the stain, because you're going to remove all the excess anyway. It also makes no difference in which direction you remove the stain, as long as you remove it all. But, it's good practice to make your last wiping strokes go with the grain, just in case you leave some streaks. That way, the streaks will be disguised by the grain.

The trick is to get all the stain wiped off the wood before it starts to dry. If you are working on a large

If you are going to wipe off all the excess stain (the most common method of applying stain), it doesn't matter in what direction you apply the stain, and it doesn't matter in what direction you remove it, as long as you remove all the excess.

surface, it's best to choose a slow-drying stain, one based on oil. Alternatively, you can divide the object into smaller parts and stain them one at a time. The parts should be divided at natural breaks, so you don't risk lap marks, as shown in the top right photo on the opposite page.

You can also leave some of the stain in order to make the wood a little darker. When removing the

TROUBLESHOOTING

USING STAIN TO REMOVE EXCESS STAIN

If a stain begins drying before you have time to get the excess removed, re-wet the wood with more stain. This will soften the existing stain so you can remove it easily.

stain, wipe in long passes with the grain, so streaking will be less likely to show. Leave as much of the excess as you like, as long as the coloring is even.

Lap marks, like those near the center of this photo, occur where a second coat of stain overlaps a first coat that has dried. To prevent them, make sure you stop staining at natural breaks in your project, or maintain a wet edge on a large surface.

The trick to removing all the excess stain is to wipe it off before it begins to dry. Otherwise, the stain will wipe off in some places and not others, causing a blotchy appearance.

Leaving the Excess

You can also apply stain and leave it all. This is more difficult than wiping off the excess, because you must apply the stain evenly to keep the color even. It's almost impossible to apply a pigment stain evenly enough using a brush or rag. A spray gun works best. But pigment-dye combinations can usually be applied successfully with a brush, as can dye stains.

Keep in mind, however, that pigment stain obscures the wood if all the excess is not wiped off. The more stain you leave on the surface of the wood, the closer the results will resemble paint. Dye is transparent, so dye stains can be applied fairly heavily on top of wood without obscuring it. Unless you intend to partially obscure the wood, it's usually best to use dye stain or pigment/dye combination stain in situations where you don't wipe off the excess, as shown in the photo below.

You may want to apply coats of dye stain and leave them in order to make the wood darker than it would get if you wiped off all the stain, or to darken sapwood to match heartwood.

In most cases, leaving an excess of a dye stain or pigment/dye combination stain (left) is more attractive than leaving an excess of a pigment stain (right). Pigment obscures the wood, so a buildup of pigment stain creates a muddy appearance.

Applying Aniline-Dye Stains

As with other finishes and stains, you can apply dye stains by wiping, brushing, or spraying. If you intend to wipe off all the excess, it won't matter which tool you use, but it may limit your choice of dyes to those that are water soluble. These are the only dyes that offer enough time to get the excess wiped off of anything but a very small surface.

If you intend to leave the dye as you apply it, spraying will produce the most even results with any type of dye. But you can also get good results brushing, especially with slow-drying water-soluble dyes. It's difficult to apply a dye stain evenly by wiping.

Brushing Dye Stains

STEP 1 The trick to brushing a dye stain is to apply it in long strokes with the grain of the wood. Continue brushing out the dye until each application is spread too thin to continue, as shown in the photo above. This evens out streaks left by your brush.

STEP 2 When the dye stain no longer spreads with your brush, re-wet the brush and resume working next to the area just brushed. Work fast enough so the previously brushed area has not fully dried before you blend it in. You must keep a wet edge or you may leave lap marks.

STEP 3 If the dye stain appears streaky or uneven when dry, dampen a cloth with the appropriate solvent and wipe with the grain over the entire surface.

To brush on a dye stain without streaking, keep brushing until each brushful of stain can't be spread any further.

This will even out the coloring and remove any streaking. If you remove too much color, replace it by brushing on another coat. (You can't remove blotchiness caused by swirly grain or uneven density in the wood this way.)

You can apply a dye stain with any type of brush. Those with natural bristles work best with all dyes, but they lose their shape fairly rapidly in water-soluble dye stains. To apply water-soluble dye stains to a large surface, you will be better off using a synthetic-bristle brush that will hold its shape. Sponge brushes will work with water-soluble dye stains but may fall apart in alcohol-soluble,

oil-soluble, and NGR (non-grain-raising) dye stains.

Spraying Dye Stains

Though you can spray any dye stain, NGR dye stains are manufactured especially for this purpose. All NGR dye stains are sold in liquid form and have one critical characteristic in common—they're in a solvent that evaporates very rapidly.

Rapid evaporation gives you control over the depth the stain will penetrate, as shown in the photo on the opposite page. If you don't want the stain to penetrate deeply, as might be the case when spraying cherry, maple, or birch— woods that have a tendency to blotch— then spray the coats lightly enough so they just barely wet the surface. The shine caused by the stain's wetness should flash off in a second or two. The faster a dye stain dries, the less time it has to penetrate.

If you want deeper penetration (in order to highlight characteristics of the wood you think attractive, for example), spray wetter

---

RIPPINGS

BRUSH TECHNIQUE
When brushing a dye stain, place each freshly loaded brush just as you would with paint—in the middle of the surface area you expect to cover, then work out to the edges from there.

coats of stain. The longer a dye stain stays wet on the surface, the deeper the stain will penetrate.

There are three ways you can control the amount of stain that you apply:

- Vary the amount of material exiting the spray gun using the gun's controls.
- Vary the distance you hold the spray gun from the wood's surface.
- Vary the speed you move the spray gun.

Spraying is the only method of applying stain that gives you control over penetration, because it allows you to deposit a fixed amount of stain everywhere. When using other methods, such as brushing or wiping, you have to wet the wood thoroughly in order to achieve even stain penetration.

Because NGR stains are meant to be sprayed and left to dry, they are supplied in a relatively weak color. You make the wood darker by spraying more coats, as shown in

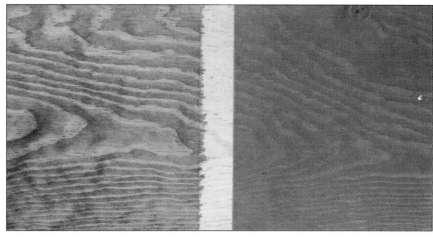

One advantage of spraying an NGR dye stain is that you can control the depth the dye penetrates. On the left, the dye was applied wet to the surface, so it soaked into the wood and blotched. On the right, the dye was sprayed in mist coats so it dried as it came in contact with the wood. Thus, it didn't penetrate and the color is much more even.

the photo below. The weaker the color, the easier it is to spray evenly, because there's less chance of building significantly more color in one spot than in another. There's also less chance of getting the wood too dark.

As weak as the supplied color is, it's almost always good practice to thin it even further. You can use methanol, denatured alcohol, or lacquer thinner. Your choice is important because it determines the evaporation rate and thus the depth that the stain will penetrate.

Methanol evaporates the fastest of these three solvents, lacquer thinner evaporates the slowest. If you want minimal stain penetration, thin the NGR dye with methanol and spray light coats. If you want deep stain penetration, thin the NGR dye with lacquer thinner and spray wet coats. Be sure to spray in an area with an exhaust system that pulls the solvent fumes away from you, or wear an organic-vapor respirator mask, as discussed on page 27.

If you do get the wood too dark, the only way to lighten it is to remove some of the dye stain by wiping with a cloth dampened with alcohol or lacquer thinner. Redissolving the stain with a wet cloth will cause the dye to penetrate deeper, however, and you may lose control of how deep the stain penetrates.

To achieve dark colors with a minimum of blotching, spray on multiple light coats of NGR stain.

Controlling Blotching

The most common and frustrating staining problem is blotching. Blotching is uneven (light and dark) coloring in woods that have swirly grain or that vary in density, as shown in the photo below. It is caused by the stain penetrating to different depths in these woods.

Blotching like this is caused by uneven stain penetration in woods with swirly grain or varying densities. Fir, pine, cherry, poplar, birch, maple, and aspen are some of the commonly used woods that typically blotch.

Blotching is difficult to predict, and it is the most serious of all finishing problems when it occurs. There is no way to remove blotching except to sand, scrape, or plane to below the depth the stain has penetrated—stain can't be totally stripped out of the wood. It is therefore very important to test the stain you are using on an incon-spicuous part or on scrap pieces from your project before committing yourself to it.

Blotching is most likely to be a problem with fir and pine, among the softwoods; and poplar, aspen, birch, and cherry, among the hardwoods. Unfortunately, these are all very popular woods, so you're likely to run into the problem frequently. Fir and pine are the most common woods used by homeowners for projects. Poplar, aspen, and birch are often chosen for making unfinished furniture. Cherry is one of the most popular woods used by serious woodworkers. If you do much wood finishing at all, it is a good idea to learn how to deal with blotching.

Preventing Blotching

To prevent blotching, the stain has to be kept from penetrating unevenly. This is done by keeping all the stain very near the surface of the wood. There are two easy ways to do this.

- Use a gel stain that doesn't flow, so it doesn't penetrate deeply into the wood.

Though thicker than liquid stains, gel stains are just as easy to apply

- Fill the pores first with a stain controller so the stain can't penetrate.

Gel Stains

Gel stains don't flow unless moved by a rag or brush, as shown in the photo above. So they barely penetrate into the wood, as shown

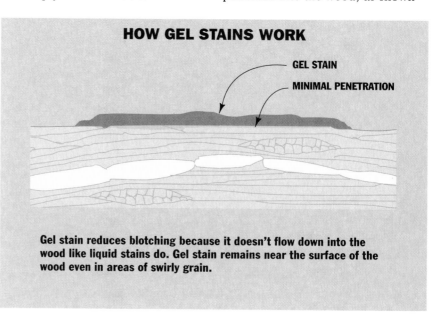

HOW GEL STAINS WORK

GEL STAIN

MINIMAL PENETRATION

Gel stain reduces blotching because it doesn't flow down into the wood like liquid stains do. Gel stain remains near the surface of the wood even in areas of swirly grain.

in *How Gel Stains Work.* The thicker the gel stain, the less it penetrates and the more effective it is at reducing or eliminating blotching. But keep in mind that while pine and cherry look better with even coloring, this effect works to a disadvantage on woods like mahogany and bird's-eye maple. With these species, you usually want deeper stain penetration to bring out the beautiful figure.

Gel stains are commonly marketed as easy to use, but this is not their real value in finishing. Their real value is reducing blotching.

Stain Controllers

Stain controllers can be used before applying a liquid stain to keep the stain from penetrating unevenly. Most stain controllers are composed primarily of slow-evaporating, petroleum-distillate solvents. They work by filling up the pores and less-dense parts of wood so the stain can't penetrate, as shown in *How Stain Controllers*

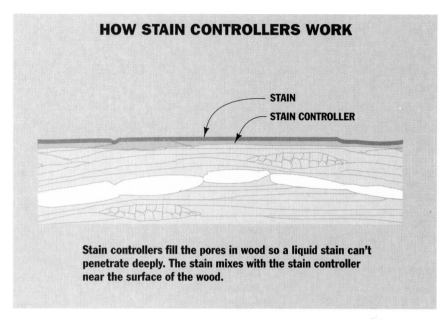

HOW STAIN CONTROLLERS WORK

STAIN

STAIN CONTROLLER

Stain controllers fill the pores in wood so a liquid stain can't penetrate deeply. The stain mixes with the stain controller near the surface of the wood.

Work. The stain just mixes with the solvent near the surface.

To get the best possible results from a stain controller, apply it liberally with a brush or rag until all parts of the wood stay wet. Keep applying more controller until no more of the liquid is absorbed into the wood. This usually takes continued applications for five to ten minutes, but the number of appli-

cations varies with the type of wood and the ingredients used in the stain controller. This advice may be contrary to what the directions on the can say. No manufacturer that I know of explains in its directions that more than one application is usually necessary.

When no more dry spots appear on the wood, wipe off all the excess stain controller and apply the stain as soon as possible—within 30 minutes is best. If you wait too long, enough of the stain controller will have evaporated or soaked deeper into the wood, so that the stain will again penetrate and cause blotching.

Which Is Best?

The effects of both gel stains and stain controllers are shown in the photo at left. Stain controllers seem to be more widely available than gel stains, and they are specifically advertised for reducing blotching. But gel stains are more predictable. They produce consistent results because there are no variables, such as number of coats applied or elapsed time before the stain is applied.

Blotching can be reduced or eliminated by using a gel stain (right) or by applying a stain controller under a liquid stain (left). Gel stains are more predictable than stain controllers because there are no variables in application.

Problem Solving
Applying Stains

There are few more frustrating aspects of finishing than staining. Perhaps this is because the results of a mistake are so visible and difficult to reverse. Here are some common problems and their solutions.

PROBLEM	SOLUTION
I applied a dye stain to a cherry table without checking to see if the wood was likely to blotch. It was, and it did. It looks pretty bad.	You can try to use solvent or paint stripper to wash out enough of the dye to make the blotching tolerable. But the only way to remove it totally is by removing all the wood to below the depth the stain has penetrated. Do this by planing, scraping, or sanding. 
I made a mirror frame that I'd like to stain, but I don't want the end grain of the pieces (which shows prominently) to be darker than the long grain.	The best way to get end grain to stain evenly is to sand it well. You should sand out all defects caused by machining, and sand to a fine enough grit so that the sanding scratches don't show. Alternatively, you can spray the stain on top of sealed wood and then not wipe off any excess. This is called toning, and it produces a different look than staining. (See "Glazing and Toning" on pages 75–76.)
I applied a lacquer-based stain to my oak tabletop, but it dried in patches before I could get all the excess wiped off. It's now dried hard.	Lacquer thinner will redissolve the stain. In fact, so will more of the stain itself, but be sure to remove all the excess before it dries. It will help if you use large cotton rags to do the wiping. Wearing gloves, soak one rag with the stain and cover the surface quickly. Then take a clean rag and promptly remove the excess. 

PROBLEM	SOLUTION
When I stained a poplar cradle I made, the stain highlighted some mill marks and some sanding scratches I thought I had sanded out.	You'll have to sand and scrape the defects out, then restain. You don't have to sand away all the color before restaining. Be sure to sand to the same grit of sandpaper you used on the rest of the cradle so the surfaces will match. Change sandpaper frequently. The stain is likely to load the paper quickly, causing it to leave a shallower scratch pattern.
While applying a water-soluble aniline dye to the side of a maple chest of drawers, I dripped some of the dye onto the lower parts. When I stained these parts, the spots didn't come out.	The darker spots are caused by the dye penetrating deeper there. Before you put on a finish, wet the side again with dye. Let it remain on the wood long enough to penetrate just as deeply as it did in the spots. They will blend in and disappear. If you get the side too dark in the process, wipe back over with a damp cloth and remove enough dye so the color is right. 
I'm making oak raised-panel doors for my kitchen. I want to finish the doors so that lighter, unstained parts don't become visible when the panels shrink.	Stain and finish the panels before you insert them into the frames. This way, no matter how much the panel shrinks, you won't see an unfinished strip along the edges. 
I was using a wiping stain on a maple end table, and it began to dry before I could get the excess wiped off. This was probably because the sun was shining on it through my open garage door. The table is now blotchy because I didn't get all the stain off.	If you had caught the problem within an hour or so, you could have softened up the stain by simply wiping over the surface with a rag containing more stain, or the thinner for the stain (I assume it is paint thinner), and then getting the excess wiped off quickly. You can still try this. If it doesn't work, you will have to use lacquer thinner or paint stripper. It won't be hard. It will probably only be necessary to dampen a cloth with the thinner or stripper and wipe over the surface. The excess stain should come right up. If you use paint stripper, be sure to follow the directions. Most strippers contain wax that has to be removed with paint thinner before you can continue finishing. Finally, remember that you shouldn't apply a finish in direct sunlight.

6
BEYOND ORDINARY FINISHING

Key Ingredients

This chapter pulls together a number of somewhat unrelated subjects, each of which will make you a better finisher. Even if you choose not to make use of the suggestions, you will find the information will help you to make more intelligent finishing decisions.

Basic finishing can be defined as simply applying a stain and finish to wood. Most handmade furniture is finished this way. But most factory furniture is finished, as shown in these photos, with additional steps that, it can be argued, give the furniture a more sophisticated look. To raise your work to this higher level, you need to know how to fill pores, use glazes and toners, and rub out a finish.

It's also helpful to understand how solvents differ from each other, since almost all finishing products make use of them. In addition, no matter how you finish your furniture, you need to know how to care for it. Even if you aren't the person who will be doing the caring, someone is sure to ask you what to do. You will feel much more comfortable with your role as a craftsman if you can give an intelligent answer.

Finishing decisions can make dramatic differences in the appearance of a particular wood. When mahogany is finished with three coats of lacquer and no pore filling (top), it has a broken surface that is relatively unattractive. Compare this effect to mahogany with the pores filled with paste-wood filler (center), and with the pores filled and the surface leveled and rubbed to a gloss (bottom).

The most perfect finish is always achieved by first leveling the surface with sandpaper, and then rubbing it to the sheen you want. Sanding can remove even the most pronounced flaws. Here, I poured the finish onto the wood and spread it around with my hand. After it cured, I sanded the right side level and rubbed it to a gloss.

You can use paste wax or furniture polish to add shine to dull surfaces. Paste wax is more effective on old surfaces that are crazed or checked. Both paste wax and liquid furniture polish are effective on surfaces in good condition.

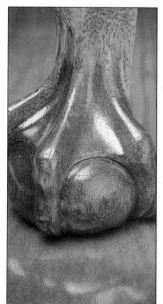

Glaze can add depth to three-dimensional objects like this ball-and-claw foot. Compare the flat look of the foot on the left to the richer look of the foot on the right. The darker areas are the result of a glaze.

A toner is a highly thinned, colored finish. It can be used to add color to an already-sealed surface or to shade objects. I have used it for both on this cherry tabletop.

Filling Pores

The pores of many woods are large enough to detract from the wood's appearance when light is reflected off the surface. This is especially the case when three or four coats of a film finish like polyurethane or lacquer are applied.

The least attractive woods are medium-pored species, such as mahogany, walnut, and teak, and large-pored species, like oak and ash. The grain pattern in medium-pored woods can be filled fairly easily to produce a mirror-flat appearance that looks more elegant. Large-pored woods are more difficult to fill successfully and attractively unless the wood is quarter-sawn. The pores in plain-sawn oak and ash are so wide that filling the pores creates large, unattractive areas of solid color.

RIPPINGS

CONTROLLING CONTRAST

Most woods darken as they age. This can create problems if you are using paste-wood filler as a stain because the filler's color will remain fairly constant. After a few years, the pores may appear lighter than the rest of the wood. In most cases, this is unattractive. By staining first, sealing, and then using a paste-wood filler that is slightly darker than the stained wood, you can ensure that the filler in the pores won't appear lighter than the wood, even if the wood darkens.

There are two ways to fill the pores in wood.
- Build up coats of finish and sand them back until the surface is level.
- Fill the pores with a grain filler before applying the finish.

Using a Finish

To use a finish to fill pores, you can either sand each coat a little after you apply it, or apply all the coats and then sand them all back together. The goal is to apply enough coats and sand them back sufficiently, so pitting is no longer visible when you look at the pores in reflected light.

The number of coats necessary to achieve a filled surface without risking sanding through depends on the size and depth of the pores

---

STEP-BY-STEP: APPLYING PASTE-WOOD FILLER

STEP 1 Thin the filler about 1½ to 2 parts thinner to 1 part filler. This makes the filler watery thin, but still thick enough to do the job. You can use either paint thinner or naphtha. Paint thinner evaporates more slowly, so it provides more time to get the filler applied and wiped off a large surface. Naphtha is usually better for use on small surfaces, since it evaporates faster.

STEP 2 Brush the filler onto the wood just as you would paint, keeping the thickness as even as possible. Then let the thinner flash off so the filler is uniformly dull over the entire surface.

in the wood you are filling, the finish you are using, and how thickly you are applying each coat. As a guide, on mahogany you will probably need 4 to 6 coats of varnish, polyurethane, or water-based finish, and 8 to 12 coats of shellac or lacquer. To get a closer idea of how many coats you will need, apply finish to your project and sand each coat back a little after it cures. Be careful not to sand through the first couple of coats.

Using Grain Filler

Grain filler is usually sold under the name "paste-wood filler." It is similar to the wood putty used to fill gouges and nail holes, in that both are made from a solid substance mixed with a

Paste-wood filler can be colored either to match the wood or contrast with it. Here, white paste-wood filler is used to give a pickled appearance to the mahogany.

STEP 3 Wipe or rub off all the excess across the grain so that filler is left only in the pores. Brands of paste-wood filler differ in their drying and hardening rates, and you may have to experiment with the type of cloth to use. A cotton cloth may do the job, but in most cases something coarser will be necessary. The coarsest commonly available cloth is burlap, which is the usual choice for removing paste-wood filler.

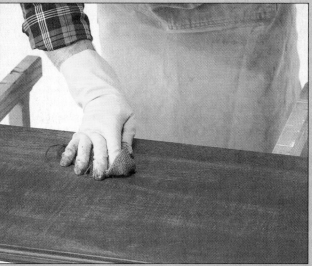

STEP 4 It is best to remove the filler by rubbing across the grain so there is less chance of pulling some of the filler out of the elongated pores. But to make sure you don't leave cross-grain streaks of paste-wood filler, finish by wiping with the grain.

binder to glue the solid particles to each other and to the wood. The solid substance in wood putty is sawdust or wood flour. In paste-wood filler it is silica, which is similar to very fine sand. The binder in wood putty is fast-curing lacquer, water-based finish, or glue, which allows you to fill relatively deep flaws in a short time. In most paste-wood fillers the binder is oil, varnish, or an oil/varnish blend that cures slowly, so you have more working time.

Like wood putty, paste-wood filler cannot be colored successfully after it has cured. So you must use a product that is supplied already colored, or add your own color to neutral paste-wood filler. You can use any of the commonly available pigments, including universal colors, japan colors, or oil colors.

You can apply the paste-wood filler directly to the wood so that it satisfies the role of both stain and filler. Or you can stain the wood first, seal it, and then apply the paste-wood filler. Either way is acceptable, but for most situations, staining and sealing before applying the paste-wood filler gives the

RIPPINGS

TO PUSH OR SLOW THE CURING

To slow the curing of an oil- or varnish-based paste-wood filler, add a little boiled linseed oil. Begin with a few drops and test until you get the curing rate you want. To speed up the curing, add japan dryer. Again, begin with just a few drops and increase the amount until the curing rate is to your liking.

RIPPINGS

USING PASTE-WOOD FILLER ON LARGE SURFACES

Applying past wood filler to a large area such a dining table top can be challenging since the filler may dry faster than you can wipe off the excess. To gain control in this situation, you should stain and seal the surface BEFORE applying the filler.

As long as you have sealed the wood before applying the paste-wood filler, you can apply it one section at a time to a large surface like a tabletop. You don't have to worry about lap marks, because you are removing all the excess filler from the surface and will be leaving it just in the pores.

most attractive and least problematic results. By applying a sealer between the stain and paste-wood filler, you create a cushion that allows you to sand off excess paste-wood filler, if necessary, with less risk of removing some of the stain color. *Applying Paste-Wood Filler* on page 72 shows the exact sequence.

No matter how level you make the surface with one coat of paste-wood filler, you can always improve the results by applying a second coat. Allow the first coat to cure a few hours in a warm room, or the second coat will just combine with it instead of building on top, and you won't get any improvement. Apply the second coat just as you did the first.

After your last coat of paste-wood filler has cured, sand it lightly with the grain of the wood

using very fine sandpaper (320-grit or finer). The purpose is to remove any cross-grain streaking that you may not have caught earlier. If you have not applied a sealer coat under the paste-wood filler, be very careful to avoid sanding through.

Remove the dust and begin applying coats of finish. You can apply any finish over paste-wood filler. But oil and oil/varnish finishes don't build, so they won't give you the filled look you are trying to achieve with paste-wood filler. And water-based finishes won't bond well to an oil- or varnish-based paste-wood filler until it is thoroughly cured.

Finish or Paste-Wood Filler?

The advantages of using the finish to fill pores are that it has less potential for causing problems, and it leaves the color of the pores close to that of the rest of the wood. The advantages of using paste-wood filler are less work, less waste, less shrinkage back into the pores over time, and the opportunity to change the color of the pores.

TROUBLESHOOTING

REMOVING HARDENED PASTE-WOOD FILLER

Brands of paste-wood filler harden at different rates. If the filler you are using gets too hard before you get it all wiped off, dampen a cloth with paint thinner or naphtha and wipe over the filler. This will soften it so you can remove it easily. If you take some of the filler out of the pores in the process, apply some more.

Glazing

Glazing is a method of applying color on top of a sealed surface to add highlights and depth to the finish. To glaze, you apply the color with any of the three basic finishing tools—rag, brush, or spray gun—and then manipulate it in some way after the thinner flashes off, moving the color around and leaving it only where you want it.

The color is carried in a product called "glaze," though common stain can be used. Glaze is a specially formulated pigment stain that is made thick so it doesn't flatten out or run on vertical surfaces. It is very similar to a gel stain.

Because glazes hold their position, the effect of your manipulation remains as you left it. In contrast, if you were to apply a liquid stain or paint thickly over a sealed surface, it would flatten out and run.

You can use the process of glazing to do the following:
- Add depth to three-dimensional surfaces like carvings, turnings, and moldings.
- Create artificial age on wood that you want to look old.
- Add color to pores without staining the wood overall.
- Create highlights in wood by applying glaze to darken the surrounding area.

You can also do graining, marbleizing, and other forms of faux finishing using glaze, but these methods are beyond the scope of this book.

Adding Depth, Age, and Color

New woodwork often looks flat when viewed from a distance, even though the surfaces may actually be three-dimensional. Eventually, however, dirt will collect in the various recesses adding depth. You can create this three-dimensional depth artificially by applying a glaze to the surface. You can also highlight the pores in wood in the same manner. This is often done with a white-pigmented glaze, a technique commonly known as pickling. The exact process is shown below in "Pickling."

Highlighting

To create highlights, apply a darker glaze to the negative areas—those parts you don't want to highlight. For example, you could apply glaze to the outside few inches of a tabletop or the panel in a raised-panel door. Feather the glaze to nothing as you work toward the center. This leaves the center of the tabletop or panel lighter.

To feather glaze successfully, use a good-quality, soft, natural-bristle brush and keep it dry when feathering out. Use a genuine glaze, and thin it with glaze extender instead of paint thinner or naphtha. You need the easy spreading characteristics of a glaze to keep from leaving brush marks.

If you are using an oil-based glaze, and you want to remove it all, you can do so for an hour or so after application without damaging the finish underneath by washing with paint thinner. There is no way to remove a water-based glaze after it has begun to set up without also removing the sealer coat—you have to use stripper.

STEP-BY-STEP: PICKLING

STEP 1 After sealing the wood with the first coat of finish (you can apply a stain under the finish), apply a glaze over the entire surface with a rag, brush, or spray gun. In many cases you can substitute a liquid stain or thinned paint successfully because the colorant doesn't have to hold its shape. It just has to color the recesses.

STEP 2 Allow the thinner to flash off so that the surface develops a haze. Then wipe off enough of the material so that it remains only in the recesses or pores. If you remove too much, just apply more. If it cures too hard to remove with a cotton cloth, substitute burlap or steel wool.

Toning

Toning is another way to add color to wood after it has been sealed. But unlike glazing, where you manipulate the color after it is on the wood, with toning you apply the color exactly where you want it, and leave it.

Toning is difficult to do successfully with a brush without leaving brush marks, so it is almost always done with a spray gun. Nothing more is involved than spraying a highly thinned, colored finish over a sealed surface, as shown on the door in the photo below left. The finish that produces the most successful results is lacquer. The colored finish should be thinned enough so that any unevenness left by overlapping strokes of the spray gun aren't noticeable. The spray gun should, of course, be adjusted to produce an even spray pattern.

Instead of spraying the toner evenly over the surface, you can create highlights and other effects by spraying only to darken certain areas. This process, shown in the photo below right, is called shading.

There is no rule governing how much to thin the colored finish, but it's better to thin too much than too little. You can always add more color. If you're using lacquer, however, you can't take color away without starting over. Begin by mixing about 1 part colorant with 1 part lacquer and thin it with 4 to 6 parts lacquer thinner. Adjust the ratio from there to get the blend you like best.

You can use either type of colorant—pigment or dye—to tone or shade. Pigment muddies the wood, so dye is usually preferred. The easiest dyes to use with lacquer are non-grain-raising dyes. (See "Aniline Dyes" on page 60.)

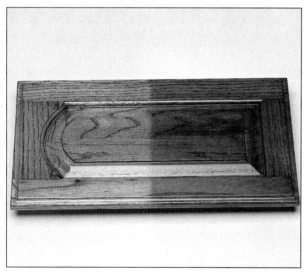

It's easy to change the color of stained wood by spraying it with a toner, after it has been sealed. In this case a red dye toner was used to make the bottom half of this door redder. If a pigment toner had been used instead, it would have muddied the wood.

By spraying a toner onto some parts and not others, you can create highlights. This technique is called shading, and the toner is sometimes called a shading stain.

PUSHING THE LIMITS: Previewing a Toner

In order to see the effect a toner will have without committing to the results, make up a mixture of japan-color pigment and naphtha and spray it onto a sealed surface. While the mixture is still damp on the surface, it will give you a good idea of the final results. If you like the effect, allow the solvent to evaporate. Then spray over the surface with a coat of finish to preserve the color. If you don't like it, wipe everything off with a cloth dampened with naphtha or paint thinner.

Rubbing a Finish

No matter how careful you are, you can't apply a perfect finish. A brush always leaves brush marks; a spray gun always leaves orange peel; there's always some dust in the air that settles in the finish. Rubbing removes these flaws, making the finish look better.

In addition, rubbing improves the tactile qualities of the finished surface. This can be a great selling point, since the first thing friends or customers do is to run their hands over a new piece of furniture. A rubbed finish will often bring comments about how good the "wood" feels. By improving both the look and feel of a finish, rubbing is the only step in finishing that can raise the quality of your work from average to special.

To overcome any fear you might have of rubbing a finish, practice first, as you did when you were learning to cut dovetails. Apply several coats of finish to a scrap piece of veneered plywood. Then rub the finish as described below. Start by trying to cut through the finish on purpose to get a feel for how much rubbing it takes. (Remember, you have to actually fall over on a bicycle a couple of times to learn how far you can lean.) Rub another part of the surface to a high gloss. Experiment with different abrasives to see what degree of polish each leaves. When you've used the entire surface, cut it back to a matte sheen with sandpaper or steel wool and start over.

Rubbing with Steel Wool

The simplest rubbed finishes are done with #0000 steel wool (or a Scotch-Brite pad if you prefer). Nothing more is involved than rubbing the surface with the grain of the wood. If the strokes are straight and you keep an even pressure, the very fine scratch marks you leave will soften and enhance the appearance and feel of the finish.

It is unlikely you will rub through to the wood if you have applied at least three coats (one sealer coat and two topcoats) of a film-building finish. But you have to be careful not to cut through the finish on edges. To avoid cutting through, rub first with short, 3-to-6-inch strokes right up to the edge, as shown in *Rubbing with Steel Wool.* It is easier to control your hand movement with short strokes than with long strokes. Connect these strokes with long strokes running the entire length of the surface, avoiding coming right up to the edge.

You can use a lubricant (soapy water, mineral spirits, mineral oil, or wax) with your steel wool to reduce the scratching a little and produce a more even sheen. But if you cut through an edge, the lubricant will disguise the raw wood and keep you from noticing the damage. You will probably continue rubbing and make the damage worse. It's better to wait to use a lubricant until you have gained some experience rubbing dry.

Rubbing with steel wool improves the appearance and feel of a finish, but it doesn't remove flaws such as brush marks, orange peel, or dust nibs. It just rounds them over. On tabletops subjected to harsh reflected light, these flaws will still be noticeable. To remove them you have to level the surface before you rub it.

Leveling with Sandpaper

You level a finish in the same way you level wood to remove machine marks and other minor flaws—by sanding with several grits of sandpaper from coarse to fine. But when sanding a finish, you begin with a much finer sandpaper (usually 400-grit or 600-grit), and you don't need to sand in the direction of the grain except with the finest-grit sandpaper you intend to use.

In fact, it's an advantage to change sanding directions with

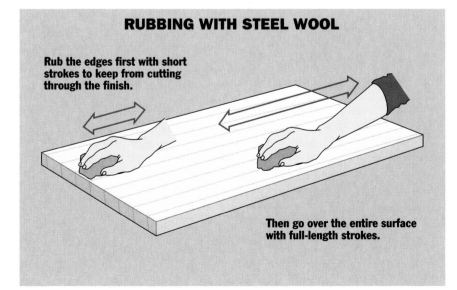

RUBBING WITH STEEL WOOL

Rub the edges first with short strokes to keep from cutting through the finish.

Then go over the entire surface with full-length strokes.

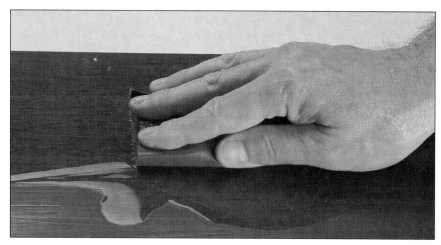

To keep the sandpaper from clogging with finish, use a lubricant—soapy water, paint thinner, mineral oil, or a mixture of paint thinner and mineral oil. I find that sandpaper still clogs too easily using soapy water, so I prefer paint thinner, mineral oil, or a mixture of the two, though many people don't like using paint thinner because of the smell.

"Two Sanding Aids" on page 6 for directions on making such a block.)Otherwise, you can use your hand to back the sandpaper. Begin sanding with 600-grit wet/dry sandpaper, as shown in the photo.

Sand until there are no more shiny spots caused by pores and other cavities. Clean off the sludge now and then to check if you've sanded enough. If 600-grit doesn't cut through the problems fast enough, drop back to 400-grit sandpaper, or to 320-grit, if even the 400-grit is too slow. Then work back up through the grits. You can stop at 600-grit if you intend to rub with steel wool or with pumice. But you will usually get better results if you sand to 1,000 grit first. (Very fine grit sandpapers and other rubbing supplies are available at auto body supply stores.)

Since you are removing much more finish when sanding it level than when simply rubbing with steel wool, the finish should be thicker to begin with or you will likely sand through. The exact

each sanding grit, even sanding in circles if you like. This way you can easily see when you have sanded enough to remove all the scratches from the previous grit of sandpaper, and you are ready to move on to the next higher grit.

If the surface is flat and you want to keep it so, back your sandpaper with a flat cork, felt, or rubber block. I use the same cork block I use for sanding wood. (See

RIPPINGS

COMPARING SHEENS
The sheen left by 600-grit sandpaper, 1,000-grit sandpaper, pumice, and #0000 steel wool is approximately the same. I find that pumice rubbed with a felt pad produces the most streak-free surface.

CHOOSING A FINISH TO RUB

The harder the film a finish can produce, the better the rubbed results will be. Also, finishes that are sold as "Gloss" as opposed to "Satin" or "Flat" will be more transparent when rubbed. Of the common film-building finishes, nitrocellulose lacquer is the easiest to rub to an even sheen and produces the most spectacular results. It is used by the furniture industry on its finest furniture.

Shellac also rubs well, as long as it is freshly made so it cures hard. But shellac shows fingerprints easily after it has been rubbed. To reduce such marking, apply paste wax.

Water-based finishes can be rubbed to an even sheen, but they don't penetrate as much as lacquer and shellac. You won't see as deeply into the wood no matter how well you rub the surface.

Varnish and polyurethane cure tough and are scratch resistant, but

they lack the hardness of lacquer and shellac. Consequently, varnish and polyurethane are more difficult to rub to an even sheen. For best results, wait a month for the finish to cure fully before rubbing.

Whichever finish you use, let it cure to the point where you can't smell any remaining solvent when you press your nose against the finish. Finishes that are rubbed before complete curing show the rubbing scratches more harshly.

number of coats will vary depending on how much of the finish you need to sand off.

Rubbing after Leveling

It's very difficult to get an even sheen using sandpaper, no matter how fine a grit you sand to. You almost always have to finish off by rubbing with #0000 steel wool or a rubbing compound. Steel wool produces a satin sheen that is much more elegant on a leveled surface than on an unleveled surface. You can use a lubricant if you wish.

For more shine, you can take the finish a step or two further with finer abrasives. Pumice and rottenstone are rubbing abrasives that

RIPPINGS

SANDPAPER FOR FINISHES

There are two types of sandpaper used to sand finishes. Both use silicon-carbide abrasive. The first type, gray or white sandpaper, contains a soaplike lubricant that reduces clogging. This sandpaper is identified by a number of names, including lubricated, no fill, and stearated (because the lubricant is a stearate). It is available in grits up to 400 and is used to sand a finish dry. It is especially useful for sanding the sealer coat when you don't want to use a lubricant because of the damage it would cause if you sanded through.

Black sandpaper is called "wet/dry" because it is made with a water-resistant glue and can be used with any type of lubricant, including water. Wet/dry sandpaper is available in grits up to 2,000. It is the sandpaper you should use when leveling a finish.

RIPPINGS

RUBBING TO A HIGH GLOSS

To achieve the ultimate high gloss after sanding the surface level, follow the procedures used by auto body refinishers. First, wet sand up to 1,500 grit. Then polish with an automotive rubbing compound and lamb's wool pad on a drill or power buffer.

Be sure to keep everything (including the air) as clean as possible. Any large grit that gets between your rubbing pad and the surface may leave a scratch deep enough to cause you to have to drop back a grit or two to remove it.

come in powder form. You mix them with water, paint thinner, or mineral oil to make a thin compound, as shown in the bottom photo. You can do the mixing in a plastic application bottle that has a pour spout, or right on the surface you are rubbing. Rub the compound using a felt block or cheesecloth wrapped tightly into a ball like a French-polishing pad. Rub in the direction of the grain. Pumice produces a satin sheen and rottenstone produces a gloss.

To make a rubbing compound using pumice or rottenstone, sprinkle some of the abrasive onto the finished surface together with a lubricant. Then begin rubbing with a felt block or a rubbing pad made of cotton or cheesecloth. The abrasive powder and lubricant will become mixed in the process.

Problem Solving
Fillers, Toners, and Glazes

Like other finishing products, fillers, toners, and glazes can be troublesome if they aren't handled properly. As always, the more you practice, the more predictable you'll find the results. Before committing your latest project to a new technique, experiment with some scraps until you become comfortable with the process.

PROBLEM	SOLUTION
Just after I applied paste-wood filler to my project, I got an emergency call. By the time I returned to the project, the filler was hard as a rock. Is there any other way to get the paste-wood filler off than sanding it? I'm afraid I'll remove part of the stain.	Stripping using a paint-and-varnish remover is the easiest way to remove the paste-wood filler. The stripper will take the filler out of the pores, so you will have to apply the filler again. The stripping may also remove some of the stain. If this happens, sand the wood lightly (to be sure all the filler is off) and then reapply the stain. It should come out even.
I applied paste-wood filler to a mahogany dining tabletop and let it cure for three days in a warm room. Then I sprayed on a coat of lacquer. The next day I noticed that the finish had raised noticeably above each pore in the mahogany. The ridges were so pronounced that I could feel them.	You applied the lacquer so wet that the lacquer thinner attacked the binder in the paste-wood filler and swelled it. It's the same phenomenon you see when you apply stripper to oil paint. The paint swells and blisters. There's probably no practical way to fix the problem now except to sand the surface level and apply more coats of lacquer. It will probably take an extra coat or two to get the surface level, because the finish will slowly sink back down into the pores. When you apply the additional coats, and when you use paste-wood filler again, apply your first couple of coats lightly enough so they don't wet the surface. Create a little buildup before you begin applying heavier, wetter coats.
I applied glaze to my raised-panel cabinet doors, followed by two coats of finish. After a short time the finish began to peel from the inside corners.	You will probably have to strip off everything and start over. You didn't let the glaze cure enough before applying the finish, and the finish wasn't able to bond well. No finish will bond to an uncured glaze. The problem may have occurred because you applied the glaze in too thick a consistency. A lot of it lodged in those inside corners lengthens the curing time considerably. Next time, thin the glaze so the build isn't as great.
I don't own a spray gun, and would like to tone wood using a brush.	You can achieve fairly successful results using a thin oil-based stain, especially one that contains both pigment and dye. The stain has to be thin (you can thin it more yourself) so it has a chance to flatten out without showing brush marks. The dye also helps to reduce brush marking.

PROBLEM	SOLUTION
When I applied a lacquer finish to a tabletop, the finish fish-eyed over a large part of the surface. I guess there was silicone oil in the wood.	You will have to strip off the finish and start over. There are two ways to prevent fish-eye. ● Seal off the silicone oil by spraying a barrier coat of freshly made shellac. (Brushing doesn't work as well because it draws the oil up into the finish.) Then apply the lacquer lightly at first so it doesn't dissolve the shellac coat. ● Add silicone oil to the finish to make its surface tension as low as that of the silicone oil in the wood. This will allow the finish to flow out evenly. Once you have added silicone oil to one coat of finish, you have to add it to each additional coat to keep the surface tension the same. Silicone oil or "fish-eye eliminator" is sold under various trade names at paint stores. Add enough silicone oil to solve the problem, usually one or two eyedropperfuls to a quart of finish. Adding such small amounts won't weaken the finish, and in fact will protect it against wear and abrasion by making it slicker. You can feel the difference in a finish that contains silicone oil.
To save time, I want to spray lacquer over an oil stain or oil-based glaze before it has totally cured. I've heard this is possible, but am concerned that it won't work well.	Spraying lacquer over a partially cured stain or glaze is possible *if* you spray at the right time. Oil stains and glazes cure by absorbing oxygen and cross-linking. But before that can happen, the thinner has to evaporate out. If you spray lacquer before the thinner has evaporated enough, the lacquer will turn milky white in the pores because the thinner throws the lacquer out of solution. You can sometimes correct this by spraying lacquer thinner or retarder onto the surface. On the other hand, if you wait until the oil or varnish binder has begun to set up, you'll get severe orange peeling. The time to spray the lacquer is right after the thinner has evaporated and the stain or glaze is dull on the surface, but hasn't yet started to set up.
Despite the care I put into it, I managed to rub through the finish on an edge of my tabletop and now the color isn't right.	The easiest way is to put the color back in with a touch-up marker. These are similar to standard felt-tip markers but they come in wood-tone colors. For larger areas, you may have to apply more stain and finish. You can apply finish to that area alone, sanding and rubbing it level with the rest of the finish, or you can add more finish to the entire surface.
I've applied paste wax to my furniture several times in the last couple of years, and now there is a smear on the surface.	Wax buildup is caused by not removing all the excess wax every time you apply it. It doesn't have anything to do with the number of times you apply wax—you could get it from only one application if you aren't careful. You can remove the buildup easily. Just rub off the excess with a clean cloth. Wax melts at around 150 degrees F so you'll have to rub hard enough to heat the surface to that temperature. You could ease the process by using a blow-dryer in combination with rubbing. It is essential that you change often to clean cloths, or you will just be moving the wax around on the surface. That may be the reason you got the buildup in the first place.

Exterior Finishes

It's much more difficult to adequately protect wood outdoors than indoors because objects outdoors are subjected more to the ravages of sun and rain. These cause splits, color loss, and even rotting. Indoors there is no rain, and what sun there is, is made less harmful by window glass.

The best way to protect wood that is left outside is to apply a coating that blocks sunlight and moisture and holds up well to these destructive elements. The best choice for long-lasting protection is paint because it stands up well to both sunlight and water.

Effects of the Sun

Light is the principal enemy of paints and finishes. Over time, ultraviolet (UV) rays from light (especially sunlight), break down paints, as shown in the photo on the opposite page. You can see this on cars and buildings that have been exposed to the sun for many years. The paint has dulled and begun to chalk.

UV rays also break down clear finishes, but most clear finishes peel before dulling and chalking become problems. The UV rays penetrate the finish film and destroy the lignin that glues the wood cells together. This causes the outermost layer of cells to separate from the rest of the wood, and the finish, which is bonded to these surface cells, peels.

The best sun-blocking agent, and thus the best UV protectorant for finishes applied outdoors, is pigment, the coloring in paint and exterior stains. Pigment blocks UV rays, so the wood underneath doesn't deteriorate. The problem with pigment is that it hides the wood. Because many

DECK FINISHES

The best way to protect a deck made of redwood, cedar, or pressure-treated wood, assuming you've ruled out paint, is with deck stain. Stains contain enough pigment to partially block UV rays. They also contain enough finish to partially block water penetration. As long as you don't build them up, stains won't peel, and you can still see the wood through them. If you like the look of water beading on your deck, use a stain that contains a water repellent. Recoat your deck about once a year for best protection.

To protect untreated pine or fir, apply a preservative to help retard rot. However, a preservative is not nearly as effective as pressure treatment and it doesn't eliminate the need for UV and moisture resistance. Some stains come with a preservative added, so you can accomplish UV resistance, moisture resistance, and rot retardance all with one product.

Water repellents cause water to bead on a deck, but they offer no protection from the sun which causes the most damage. The best way to protect a deck, other than painting it, is to apply a pigmented stain. The pigment partially blocks UV rays, and the binder in the stain retards water penetration.

people want to see the natural wood, they don't want to use paint or stain.

The next best sun-blocking agents are UV absorbers. These chemicals are similar to the active ingredients of sunscreen lotions. They convert UV light energy to heat energy, which dissipates. UV absorbers don't hide wood, and they are fairly effective at preventing wood deterioration under a finish.

The problem with UV absorbers is that they are very expensive, and a significant amount—1 to 3 percent by weight—has to be included in the finish to be effective. It isn't enough to add just a few drops to a vat so it can be claimed that the product contains UV absorbers.

The most common finishes that contain sufficient UV absorbers are marine varnishes. These varnishes cost from $50 to $100 a gallon and are usually available only from suppliers that cater to the boat building trade. As a result, there are very few situations where using one of these varnishes is a realistic alternative. If you still insist on using a clear film finish outdoors and don't

All exterior finishes must be maintained and renewed periodically. Done regularly, all that's required is a light sanding and recoating. Once a finish starts to peel, however, your only recourse is to strip it and start over.

want to spend the money for a marine varnish, use a spar varnish knowing that you may have to remove and replace it often.

Effects of Moisture

Moisture causes finishes to peel when it gets between the finish and the wood. Moisture can penetrate directly through the finish film, or it can penetrate through a crack in the film and work its way through the wood cells. Again, the best water resistance is provided by paint, and

by spar and marine varnishes that are made to be very flexible, so they keep up with extreme wood movement.

There are several finishes, including oil, shellac, and to some degree, lacquer, that do not resist moisture penetration well. Rain causes these clear finishes to peel or disintegrate fairly rapidly. Water repellents, which contain low-surface-tension waxes or silicone oils, provide some moisture resistance and they don't peel, but they are short-lived and have to be reapplied regularly.

CHOOSING A PAINT

Paint performs well outdoors because it repels water and blocks UV rays very effectively. There are two major categories of paint: oil-based and water-based (latex). Oil-based paints are better for objects such as chairs and picnic tables because they wear better than latex paints. Oil-based primers are also best if you are painting wood that has been exposed to the weather for a month or more, because they

penetrate deeper than latex primers. (Exposure breaks down the surface cells making it difficult for paint to get a good hold.) If the wood is freshly milled or sanded, acrylic-latex primers perform well. No primer is necessary over old paint or finish that is still in good shape.

Latex paint is best for wood siding, because it allows moisture vapor to pass through better than oil paint does. What seems to be a deficiency is actually a benefit

because moisture that is generated inside buildings from cooking, showers, etc. has to be able to get out when the building is closed up for heating or air conditioning. The moisture works its way through the walls, insulation, and wood siding. If it can't get through the paint, it builds up behind the paint and causes the paint to peel. A primer coat of oil-based paint is not thick enough to stop the penetration, and will also allow the moisture to escape.

Solvents

Finishing couldn't be done without solvents. Even if you use only water-based products, you can't avoid solvents because they are included in almost all water-based stains and finishes. And solvents can be used to handle many problems. So it's important that you know a little about solvents and how they relate to each other.

Solvents are grouped in families. Each family reacts with a finish in a different way. Within each family, solvents differ primarily in evaporation rate; solvents with smaller molecules evaporate faster than those with larger molecules. The best-known family to illustrate this relationship is the hydrocarbon family.

Hydrocarbon Solvents

Hydrocarbons are distilled from petroleum and are composed entirely of hydrogen and carbon. They are used in finishing primarily to thin and clean up oil- and varnish-based products.

Three common hydrocarbon liquids are available in paint stores—naphtha (also sold as benzine), paint thinner (mineral spirits), and kerosene. (Turpentine, or turps, is an equivalent solvent to paint thinner; however, it is distilled from pine-tree sap instead of petroleum.) Of these, naphtha contains the smallest molecules, so it evaporates the fastest. The molecules in kerosene are so large that they don't evaporate well at all. Kerosene is therefore not useful as a finishing solvent.

As the molecules in the liquid become larger, the liquid becomes more oily. Paint thinner is oilier

---

than naphtha, and kerosene is oilier than paint thinner. Finally, the distilled product is so oily that it is classified as an oil. One of the hydrocarbon oils most familiar to woodworkers is mineral (paraffin) oil.

Because none of these distillations damages finishes, and because oily substances are effective at picking up dust and adding shine to dull surfaces, petroleum-distillate solvents are widely used as the main ingredient in furniture polishes.

Benzene (benzol), toluene

(toluol), and xylene (xylol) are also taken from petroleum. These solvents are very dry (non-oily) and fast evaporating. Benzene was once widely used in finishing as a solvent and paint stripper. But it is used no longer, because it is now known to be carcinogenic.

Toluene and xylene are used primarily as cleaners to remove oily substances from metal and wood. These solvents can also be used to soften white and yellow glue, water-based finish, and latex paint. Xylene is used in products sold in paint stores for cleaning latex paint spatter off of furniture without damaging the finish. Of course, these products will damage water-based finishes.

The distillations that become naphtha and paint thinner contain very small amounts of benzene, toluene, and xylene. When these are removed, what is left is fairly odorless, and it is sold as odorless mineral spirits. Odorless mineral

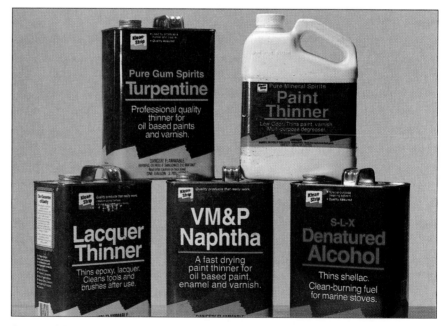

Along with the various wood finishes on the market are a collection of solvents used for thinning and cleaning up. The five solvents most commonly used by woodworkers are pictured here.

spirits doesn't have quite the solvent strength of regular paint thinner; however, it is usually strong enough to thin varnish and polyurethane. You can tell if it isn't strong enough because the finish and the thinner will separate after stirring.

Other Families

Other common families of solvents are alcohols, ketones, and esters.

Alcohols are used for many purposes, including the following:

- For thinning and stripping shellac
- For thinning non-grain-raising (NGR) dye stains
- For drying off strippers based on di-basic esters and n-methyl pyrrolidone
- For an ingredient in lacquer thinner and in most paint-and-varnish removers

Methanol is the fastest-evaporating alcohol. It is the best alcohol to use for thinning NGR dye stains, because the fast evaporation rate allows you to control the depth of stain penetration.

But methanol is very toxic, so it should be used only when adequate exhaust is available. Organic-vapor respirator masks are not very effective at blocking methanol.

Ethanol is the most commonly available alcohol in paint stores. It is sold as denatured alcohol, which is ethanol with a poisonous solvent added so the product isn't taxed as a liquor. Denatured alcohol (also called shellac thinner) is the alcohol you should use in all situations when you can't exhaust the fumes.

Rubbing alcohol, sold in pharmacies, contains too much water to be useful in finishing.

Ketones and esters dissolve lacquer and are the active solvents in lacquer thinner. Acetone and methyl ethyl ketone (MEK) are the smallest ketone molecules and thus the least oily and fastest-evaporating. They are often available in paint stores and are used primarily for removing oil or grease from metal and wood. Ester solvents are not commonly available.

To make lacquer thinner, manufacturers choose between ketones and esters primarily for their particular evaporation rates. For example, slower-evaporating ketones and esters are chosen for use in lacquer retarder. Faster-evaporating ketones and esters are chosen for use in fast-drying lacquer thinner.

Because only about 40 percent of lacquer thinner needs to be a ketone or ester, methanol and toluene are added to reduce cost. Methanol acts synergistically with the active solvents to dissolve the lacquer. Toluene dilutes or thins the lacquer thinner, and it evaporates very fast, so it helps reduce lacquer runs and sags on vertical surfaces.

FINISHES AND THEIR THINNERS

FINISH	COMMON THINNER
Wax	Paint Thinner/Turpentine
Oil/Oil-Varnish Blends	Paint Thinner/Turpentine
Varnish/Polyurethane	Paint Thinner/Turpentine
Shellac	Denatured Alcohol
Lacquer	Lacquer Thinner
Water-Base	Water

Caring for Furniture

Furniture deteriorates primarily because of moisture exchange between the wood and the atmosphere. When the surrounding air is drier than the wood, the wood loses moisture and shrinks. When the surrounding air is wetter than the wood, the wood absorbs moisture and swells. Excessive shrinkage and swelling causes warps, splits, joint failure, and veneer peeling.

The best way to slow wood movement is to maintain the humidity at a constant level. Museums do this to preserve their furniture collections, but for most homeowners the best alternative is to keep the finish on the furniture in good shape. A finish slows moisture exchange so that potential problems take much longer to develop.

How to Maintain a Finish

The two most damaging elements to a finish are physical abuse and light, especially sunlight. Consider how much faster paint deteriorates on the south side of a house than on the north side. But even indoor lighting eventually takes its toll on a finish. You can confirm this by removing hardware from furniture that is 40 years old or more. The newly exposed finish will be in far better shape than the surrounding finish. Neither paste wax nor liquid furniture polish obstructs the penetration of light.

To protect a finish against damage caused by light, shield the finish by placing furniture away from direct sunlight, turn the lights off in rooms when they are not occupied, keep tabletops covered when not in use, and throw a sheet over particu-

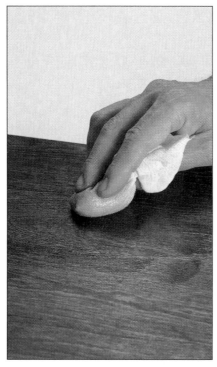

To apply paste wax to a finish, put some wax inside a cloth so it seeps through as you rub the surface. When the wax hazes, rub off the excess with a clean cloth. Keep turning the cloth or replacing it with a clean one so you remove the excess wax rather than just move it around.

larly vulnerable furniture when you're on vacation.

Physical abuse can be anything that breaks the finish film, from gouges and scratches to damage from heat, solvents, acids, or alkalis (like soap). To protect a finish from physical abuse, use coasters, tablecloths, and hot pads, and discipline your children and pets. You can also get some benefit from using wax or furniture polish.

Wax and Furniture Polish

Waxes and liquid furniture polishes perform five functions:
- Add shine to dull surfaces, as shown in the photo above.
- Provide scratch resistance by reducing friction

- Aid in picking up dust
- Clean away dirt
- Add scent to a room

All five functions are of value, but only one, reducing friction, is directly protective.

Wax doesn't evaporate, so liquid and paste waxes provide fairly permanent shine and scratch resistance. But, because there is no need to apply it often, wax is ineffective at removing dust, cleaning dirt, or adding scent.

Liquid furniture polishes are based primarily on oily petroleum-distillate solvents in the range between paint thinner and kerosene. They provide shine and scratch resistance only until they evaporate. Some polishes evaporate faster than others so the duration of protection varies.

The problem is you can't have shine and scratch resistance using a liquid without also having smear. As long as the oily solvent remains on the surface, it will be smeary. When the smear is gone, so is the oily solvent, and with it the shine and scratch resistance. So, unless you are willing to live with smeary furniture, liquid furniture polishes are not effective at providing shine and scratch resistance. The real benefit of liquid furniture polishes is in picking up dust, cleaning dirt, and adding a pleasant scent to a room.

Dampening a cloth with furniture polish helps the cloth pick up dust instead of just moving it around. But remember that the oily solvent in furniture polish is a petroleum distillate. It will remove wax. Don't apply liquid furniture polish over wax unless you intend to remove it.

Petroleum-distillate solvents dissolve grease, so furniture polishes make good grease removers. But these solvents don't remove water-soluble dirt, like that left by children's sticky fingers. So, many manufacturers also market a water-emulsified furniture polish that is a combination of solvent and water, and capable of cleaning both solvent- and water-soluble dirt. You can identify these polishes, as shown in the photo at right, by their milky white color. Furniture polishes based on oily solvent alone are clear.

In general, neither wax nor liquid furniture polish causes any harm to a finish that is in good shape. You don't need to fear that you are damaging your furniture no matter which wax or furniture polish you use.

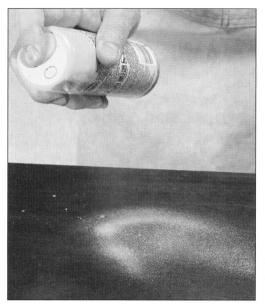

Furniture polishes are made of either an oily solvent or an emulsification of oily solvent and water. Emulsified furniture polishes are milky white and clean water-soluble dirt, in addition to grease. Non-emulsified furniture polishes are clear and don't clean water-soluble dirt. Use an emulsified polish for more complete cleaning. Use a solvent furniture polish on old, fragile surfaces where you don't want water getting underneath the finish through cracks.

THE ISSUE OF SILICONE-OIL FURNITURE POLISHES

Some furniture polishes—like Pledge—contain silicone oil. Silicone oil is an inert, synthetic oil that is very much like mineral oil. Because it is inert, silicone oil doesn't react with, or cause damage to anything. This is important because polishes containing silicone oil are often falsely accused of causing all sorts of damage to finishes. This just isn't true.

Polishes that contain silicone oil perform all five of the functions of furniture care products admirably. And because silicone oil doesn't evaporate, its benefits are fairly long lasting.

The trouble with silicone oil comes with refinishing. If any of the oil gets through the finish and into the wood, it causes a newly applied finish to not flow out well. Usually, the silicone oil remains in the pores of wood and keeps the finish from flowing over these pores, causing craters known as "fish eyes," as shown in the photo.

If you try to finish over wood that has silicone oil in the pores, the finish is likely to form fish eyes where the silicone oil prevents it from flowing out. While fish eyes are a nuisance, they can be dealt with and are not a reason to worry about using furniture polish containing silicone oil.

Distressing Wood

Old furniture and woodwork look different than new furniture and woodwork largely because of color change, wear, and the accumulation of dirt in recesses. The procedure for imitating the appearance of age on new wood is called "distressing."

There is no single right way to do distressing. Every situation is different, and a lot depends on the look you are trying to imitate. Therefore, it's more valuable to understand the broad methods of distressing then it is to concentrate on specific step-by-step procedures. This way, you can choose the specific steps and techniques that will produce the exact look you want.

Color Change

All woods change color as they age. Most darken, but a few, such as walnut, become lighter. Other woods lighten because they are bleached by the sun. The best way to approximate these color changes is with stains and bleaches.

Dye stains usually work better than pigment stains. Dye stains color wood more evenly and naturally than pigment stains which highlight pores, grain, and other recesses by lodging in them and making them darker. Pigment added to a finish and applied as a toner tends to muddy the wood; dye toners don't. Though using pigment may produce a pleasing result, it is seldom the same as wood that has aged.

New wood can also be lightened artificially with two-part bleach—a combination of sodium hydroxide (lye) and hydrogen peroxide—as shown in the photo. Thin the bleach with water to achieve various degrees of lightening, then stain the wood back to the color you want.

It's always wise to practice coloring scrap wood before applying stain or bleach to the actual project, so you get an idea of what will happen. Changing a stain color, or replacing a bleached-out color, is often difficult.

Wear

Distressing is most often thought of as beating furniture with chains or other metal objects. Beating furniture is one way to fake wear in furniture, but there are other, more subtle ways of going about it. Wear can take many forms, and the trick to making artificial wear look convincing is to make it look natural. See the photo on the opposite page.

The trouble with chains and other common distressing "tools" is they tend to make nearly identical ding marks. But the dings and gouges made over 100 years of use would be nowhere near identical. Furthermore, as a piece of furniture is used, wood can actually be worn away on parts like chair rungs and edges of tabletops. This type of wear can be better imitated using rasps, sandpaper, and wire brushes.

The best way to determine the type of wear to add to new furniture is to look at old furniture and notice how it has been dinged and worn. Then choose the tools or objects that will most closely create the same effects. Most importantly, don't make the same marks all over. Think of a piece of furniture as having spent a generation of

To use two-part bleach, wet the wood with one of the two solutions. (It doesn't matter which chemical you use first.) Before the first chemical dries, brush on a coat of the second solution. Be sure to protect your hands and eyes—bleach burns. Allow the wood to dry, then rinse it with white vinegar to neutralize any remaining lye.

ings, and moldings, as shown in the photo on page 90. In some cases, what has actually happened is that much of the finish has been worn away from the high spots from use or frequent polishing. With either situation, the effect is the same: The recesses are darker.

You can imitate this effect easily by glazing. (See "Glazing" on page 75.) Any oil or water-based stain (or paint thinned to the consistency of stain) can be used as a glaze, or you can use a special glaze product which is formulated to spread and be manipulated easier than stain or thinned paint.

Apply a wet coat of glaze over a sealed surface with a rag, brush, or spray gun, let the thinner flash off so the glaze loses its shine, then wipe most or all of the glaze off the high spots leaving it in the recesses to simulate dirt. Allow the glaze time to cure, then apply at least one more coat of finish to protect the glaze from being scratched or rubbed off.

Oil-based glazes or stains are easier to use than water-based glazes or stains because oil-based products dry much slower. You have more time to manipulate them to achieve the look you want. On the other hand, you can coat over water-based glazes much sooner, and they don't fill the air with so much solvent smell.

Probably the single biggest mistake people make in using glaze to simulate dirt is not thinning the glaze enough and getting too thick of a build. The dirt buildup in recesses of old furniture is usually very thin.

In most cases the color you should use to simulate dirt is dark brown or walnut. The most popular earth colors for this step are

Notice where wear commonly occurs on old furniture. Chair rungs, where people often rest their feet, are typical examples. Imitate this wear with stain or glaze followed by abrading with sandpaper, a rasp, or a wire brush.

time in each of several different households, some treating their furniture with care, others roughly.

It's always a good idea to practice before trying something on a project in which you've invested a great deal of time. Take a fairly large scrap of wood, and try to make it look natually worn. Use the butt ends of various kitchen utensils and woodworking tools, and use rasps, sandpaper and a wire brush to soften and wear edges. Try distressing before you apply a stain and finish, and then do the distressing on top of a stain and finish to see the difference.

Dirt

Old furniture often has dust and dirt accumulated in recesses such as those on carvings, turn-

Van Dyke brown and burnt umber. You can add these colors to neutral glaze to make your own colored glaze.

Other Tricks

Beyond adding (or subtracting) color, glazing, and hastening wear and tear, there are many other tricks you can use to make a piece of furniture look old. Again, consider how a piece of furniture might have been used, then try to mimic such use. Throw your keys casually on top of a chest of drawers. Set a heavy box on a tabletop, then drag it slightly as you lift it off. Water rings, cigerette burns, even carved initials are all fair game. Some professional distressors even leave furniture out in the weather to accelerate the seasonal expansion and contraction across the grain.

Or you may choose a different approach—just finish the piece and leave it alone. In one hundred years or so, it will have accumulated all the character of a genuine antique.

It's common for recesses in carvings, turnings, and moldings to collect dirt while the stain and finish get worn off high spots. You can imitate this look by applying a glaze and then wiping the excess off the high areas, or abrading it off with steel wool.

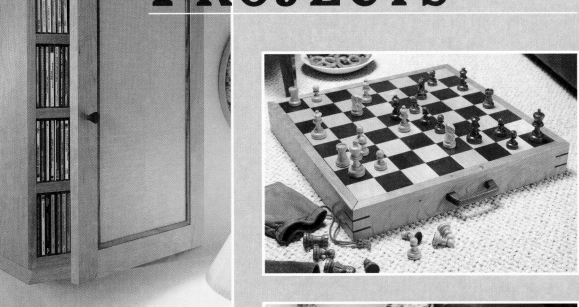

PROJECTS

DISPLAY-TOP COFFEE TABLE

Old campaign buttons, model racing cars, even antique tools will look right at home in your living room when housed in the top of this coffee table. With its polished finish, the table should fit right into the finest of settings.

Do you have collectibles languishing in a box for lack of a suitable way to display them? Why not build them a proper home so you can have them out to enjoy?

The beauty of a display-top coffee table is that it serves more than one purpose. Thus, you can show off your collection of tiddly winks and swizzle sticks on Saturday night and still have a place to spread out

the paper come Sunday morning. As a bonus, the display area is relatively dust-proof, so you won't have to spend much time on upkeep the way you would with a wall-hung display.

Access to the bin is simple, yet not obvious. A small hole hidden under the felt liner allows you to poke a pencil up through the display to lift the glass. This keeps your treasures safe from all but the most inquisitive (or those who carry bricks).

The table is solidly built of mahogany, with mortise-and-tenon joints throughout. The finish is downright elegant. It starts with a deep red stain to give the wood a rich color. This is followed by a sealer coat of thin varnish, two coats of dark paste-wood filler, and several coats of polyurethane varnish. This combination of filler and varnish leaves a glass-smooth surface that is exceptionally durable.

Procedure

1 Cut the leg joinery. Cut the legs and aprons to the sizes listed in the Materials List. Join the pieces with mortise-and-tenon joints, as shown in the *Leg Joinery Details.* For more details on cutting mortises and tenons, see "Cutting Mortise-and-Tenon Joints" on page 98. Also, cut dadoes partway across the long aprons to hold the partitions, as shown.

2 Taper the legs. After mortising, taper the two inside faces of each leg on the table saw with the help of a tapering jig, as shown in **Photo 1.**

3 Assemble the base. Glue and clamp the aprons to the legs. Check to make sure the assembly is square by measuring the diagonals. (They should be equal.) While the glue is setting, cut the corner braces to the size listed and bevel the ends at 45 degrees. Screw and glue the braces to the inside corners with 1¼-inch screws, as shown in **Photo 2.**

4 Make the display bin. Cut the partitions and the ledgers to the sizes listed. Rabbet the ends of the partitions to create tongues that fit in the grooves that you cut in the long aprons. Cut away part of each tongue to accommodate the area where the groove stops. Glue the partitions in place. Glue and screw the ledgers along the lower edge of the partitions and the long aprons with ¾-inch screws.

Cut a piece of plywood to fit within the frame to form the bin bottom, but don't glue it in place—you'll want it to be removable so you can replace the lining if necessary. Drill a 5⁄16-inch hole near one corner, as shown in *Top View* on page 95, for access to pop the glass out when needed. Set the bottom aside until later.

LEG JOINERY DETAILS

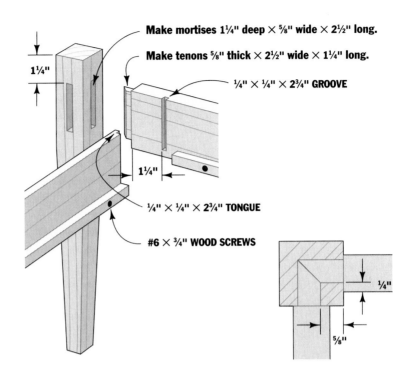

Make mortises 1¼" deep × ⅝" wide × 2½" long.

Make tenons ⅝" thick × 2½" wide × 1¼" long.

¼" × ¼" × 2¾" GROOVE

1¼"

1¼"

¼" × ¼" × 2¾" TONGUE

#6 × ¾" WOOD SCREWS

¼"

⅝"

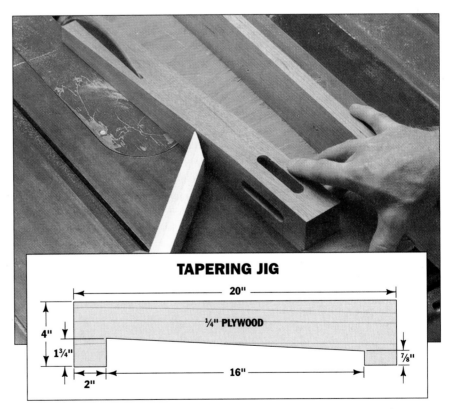

TAPERING JIG

20"

¼" PLYWOOD

4"

1¾"

16"

⅞"

2"

Photo 1: **Set the rip fence so the taper starts just under the point where the aprons join the legs. Push on the leg to propel both the leg and the jig through the cut.**

EXPLODED VIEW

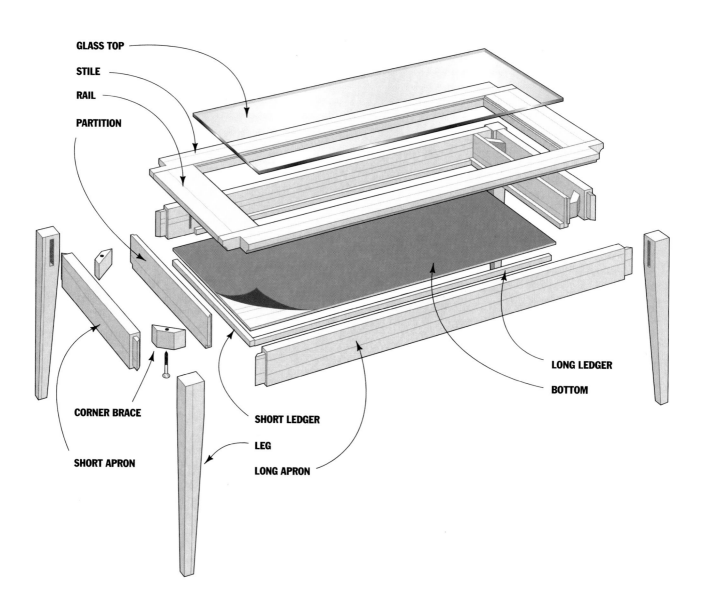

GLASS TOP

STILE

RAIL

PARTITION

LONG LEDGER

BOTTOM

CORNER BRACE

SHORT LEDGER

LEG

SHORT APRON

LONG APRON

TOP VIEW

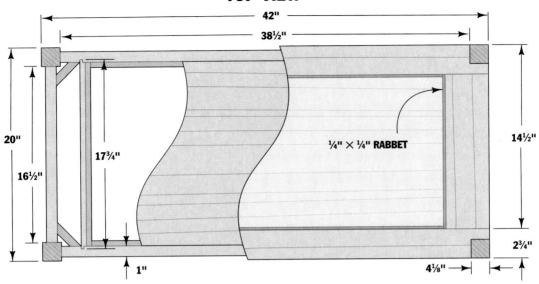

¼" × ¼" RABBET

42"
38½"
20"
16½"
17¾"
14½"
2¾"
1"
4⅛"

FRONT VIEW

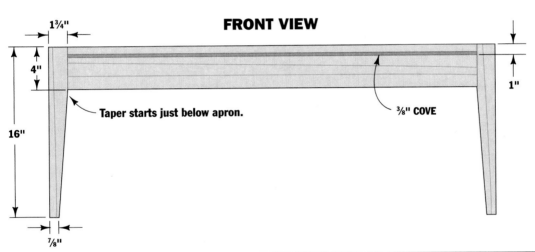

1¾"
4"
16"
7/8"
1"
Taper starts just below apron.
⅜" COVE

MATERIALS LIST

PART	QTY.	DIMENSIONS	PART	QTY.	DIMENSIONS
Legs	4	1¾" × 1¾" × 16"	Stiles	2	1" × 2¾" × 42"
Long aprons	2	1" × 3" × 41"	Rails	2	1" × 4⅛" × 18½"
Short aprons	2	1" × 3" × 19"			
Corner braces	4	¾" × 1½" × 2⅝"			
Partitions	2	½" × 3" × 17¾"			
Short ledgers	2	½" × ½" × 17¼"			
Long ledgers	2	½" × ½" × 33"			
Bottom (plywood)	1	¼" × 17¼" × 34"			

HARDWARE

Glass top ¼" × 15" × 34¼"

#6 × 1¼" brass flathead wood screws (8)

#6 × ¾" brass flathead wood screws (24)

#8 × 2" brass flathead wood screws (4)

#6 × ½" brass flathead wood screws (4)

Felt 24" × 36"

5 Make the top. Cut the stiles and rails to size. Join them with mortise-and-tenon joints, as shown in *Frame Detail.* Glue and clamp the frame together. After the glue dries, rout a rabbet around the inside of the frame to hold the glass, as shown. Square the rabbet at the corners with a sharp chisel. Rout a ³⁄₈-inch cove around the underside of the frame, leaving the edge about ⁵⁄₈ inch thick.

6 Fit the top. On the band saw, cut away the corners of the frame to fit around the legs. File or pare the notches to a perfect fit. In making these notches, don't be surprised when you cut into the mortise-and-tenon joints. They'll be concealed again once the frame is installed. Carefully round-over the top edges of the frame, as well as the top edges of the leg, with sandpaper to create a slight shadow line between the pieces. Screw the top to the base through the corner braces with 2-inch screws.

7 Apply the stain and filler. Go over the table carefully with sandpaper to make sure all the surfaces are as refined as possible. Then wipe on a coat of pigment or dye stain. The table in the photos was stained with a dark red mahogany, oil-based, dye-pigment stain. Keep in mind that because the inside of the bin will be visible, you must finish it nicely, too.

Once the stain dries, seal the surfaces with a thin coat of varnish (varnish mixed 50/50 with paint thinner), or a varnish-based sanding sealer. Allow the sealer coat to dry, but don't sand afterward—you don't want to risk sanding through. Instead, apply a coat of dark pastewood filler, thinned to a watery consistency. Wipe off the excess after the solvent flashes off. Apply a second coat of filler after the first coat has dried thoroughly (several hours minimum). After the second coat of filler has dried, sand the surface

Photo 2: Corner braces add an amazing amount of strength to a table frame. They also provide a handy place to attach the tabletop.

FRAME DETAIL

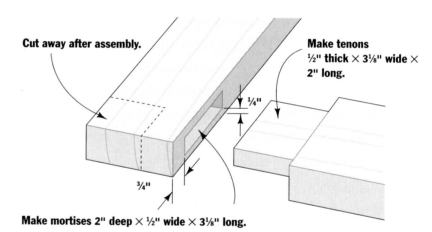

Cut away after assembly.

Make tenons ½" thick × 3⅛" wide × 2" long.

¼"

³⁄₄"

Make mortises 2" deep × ½" wide × 3⅛" long.

with 400-grit sandpaper to smooth any irregularities and remove streaks.

8 Apply the finish. Carefully wipe the table down to remove all traces of dust, and clean up your shop thoroughly before applying the top coats of varnish. Some woodworkers even wet the floor down to keep from raising dust when finishing. Wait for an hour or so to allow the dust to settle before proceeding.

Brush on a coat of polyurethane with an ox-hair brush. (A good quality china-bristle will work almost as well.) Allow the finish to dry according to the instructions on the can, then sand the table smooth with 400-grit sandpaper. Apply a second coat, and sand as before. A third coat may be necessary,

but two may be okay. Rub out the finish with a mixture of pumice and mineral oil. This will take the table to a satin glow. For a higher gloss, get some automotive rubbing compound and polish the table with a lamb's-wool buff.

9 Finish up. Purchase a piece of glass to fit the opening in the top frame. Have the glass cutter polish the edges and slightly round the corners for you. Cut a piece of felt the same size as the bottom. Spread the felt smoothly over the bottom (iron out any wrinkles) and glue it in place around the edges with a thin bead of white glue. Leave a small flap of felt unglued at each corner so you can fold the felt back to screw the bottom to the table with ½-inch screws.

Design Variations

With any piece of furniture, it is the details that provide a sense of style and presence. True, the dimensions and proportions of the piece play an important role in how good it looks, but the details are what really determine its character. Once you have the details set, you can vary the dimensions, making the piece bigger or smaller to suit your purposes.

Consider the Display-Top Coffee Table, shown on page 92. It has three distinctive details that make up its "look":

- Tapered legs that pierce the tabletop
- A cove along the underside of the top, to lighten its appearance

- Inset aprons

By keeping to these details and playing with the dimensions, you can make any number of related pieces, perhaps to fill out a suite of furniture.

Obviously, lengthening the aprons will make a larger coffee table. But, by changing no more than the length of the legs, you can also create a matching sofa table or library table. Such a table should have legs from 28 to 32 inches long. A table with even longer legs (to 36 inches) might find a home in the foyer.

No matter what the height, you could also add a shelf underneath and still have a table that relates well to the original design. The shelf could be a solid piece of wood, or a frame

with a glass panel. (To install a shelf, cut shallow dadoes across the inside corners of the legs and slip the shelf in place at glue-up.)

Also, keep in mind that working within a given set of details doesn't mean you can't make major changes. Any of the tables being discussed would look fine with a solid-wood top rather than glass. They would be simpler to build as well, since there would be no need for the inner bin. If you choose to go with a solid top, be sure to leave a little clearance around the tops of the legs so the tabletop will be able to expand and contract with changes in the weather.

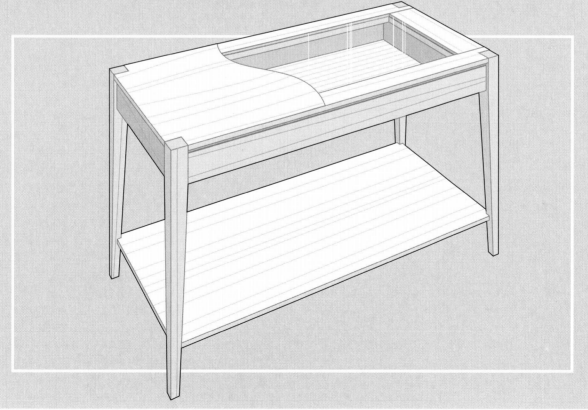

SHOP SOLUTIONS: Cutting Mortise-and-Tenon Joints

It's tough to do much wood-working without stumbling across the mortise-and-tenon joint. It is the key connection for building sturdy tables and warp-free doors. Because it is the joint of choice in so many situations, it's worth developing reliable jigs and techniques for cutting the mating parts accurately. Make the mortises first, then cut the tenons to fit.

Cutting Mortises. In the small shop, the plunge router has become the mortising tool of choice. Equipped with an adjustable edge guide, a plunge router can churn out accurate mortises in a matter of seconds. The bit diameter is equal to the width of the mortise. A regular straight bit will work, but a spiral-upcut bit makes a cleaner cut.

If you only have a few mortises to cut, lay out the ends of each mortise individually. If you have a lot of mortises to make, it's worth the effort to clamp stop blocks in place to locate both the stock and the mortise.

For mortises in fairly thick (about 2 inches) stock, you can run the router along the edge of the stock itself. For mortises in thinner material, clamp the pieces to the edge of a wider board to provide a little extra support, as shown in the photo at left.

Routing produces mortises with rounded ends. You can either square the ends with a chisel, or round-over the corners of the tenons with a file. Either way works. Try both methods to see which you find to be easier.

Cutting Tenons. Tenons are more complicated to make than mortises. But they can still be cut on the table saw without a struggle by making up the tenoning jig shown in *Tenoning Jig* on the opposite page. The jig holds the workpiece in a vertical position as you run it past the

STEP-BY-STEP: CUTTING A TENON ON THE TABLE SAW

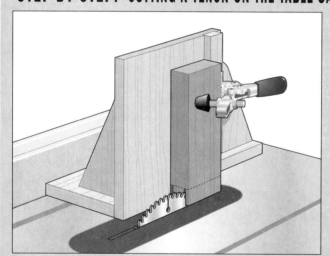

STEP 1 Adjust the rip fence to position the stock. Cut the cheek farthest from the fence first.

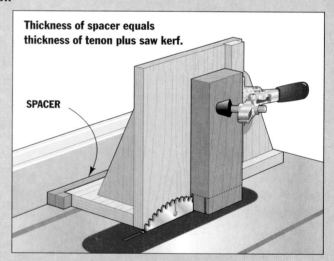

Thickness of spacer equals thickness of tenon plus saw kerf.

SPACER

STEP 2 Fit the spacer between the jig and fence, then cut the second cheek.

blade. The spacer determines the tenon thickness. This spacer may seem like overkill at first, but once you've made and sized the spacer to match your mortising bit (masking tape makes a handy shim), you can set up to cut a few tenons with very little effort. The procedure is shown in "Cutting a Tenon on the Table Saw".

Note: Many woodworkers cut tenons by making one cheek cut, then reversing the workpiece in the jig to cut the second side. True, this procedure eliminates the need for the spacer and it centers the tenon on the workpiece. But it also makes setting up the jig a trial each and every time you want to tenon, since every adjustment you make to the saw fence is doubled on the workpiece.

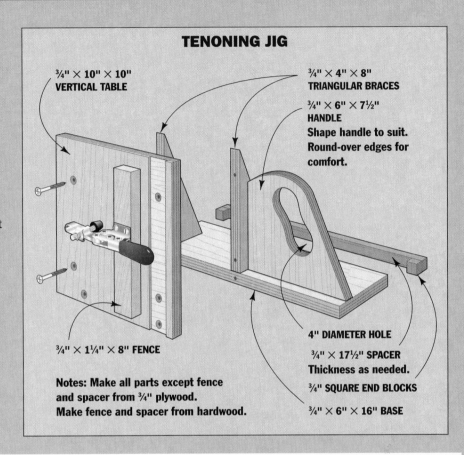

TENONING JIG

¾" × 10" × 10" VERTICAL TABLE

¾" × 4" × 8" TRIANGULAR BRACES

¾" × 6" × 7½" HANDLE
Shape handle to suit. Round-over edges for comfort.

¾" × 1¼" × 8" FENCE

4" DIAMETER HOLE

¾" × 17½" SPACER Thickness as needed.

¾" SQUARE END BLOCKS

¾" × 6" × 16" BASE

Notes: Make all parts except fence and spacer from ¾" plywood. Make fence and spacer from hardwood.

Tip clamp out of the way.

STEP 3 Move the clamp and reposition the fence to cut the tenon edges. Hold the piece in the jig securely with your hands as you make the cuts.

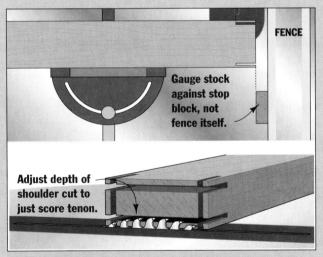

FENCE

Gauge stock against stop block, not fence itself.

Adjust depth of shoulder cut to just score tenon.

STEP 4 Saw the shoulders by guiding the stock past a crosscut blade with the miter gauge. Use a stop block along the rip fence to help position your piece.

COMPACT DISC CABINET

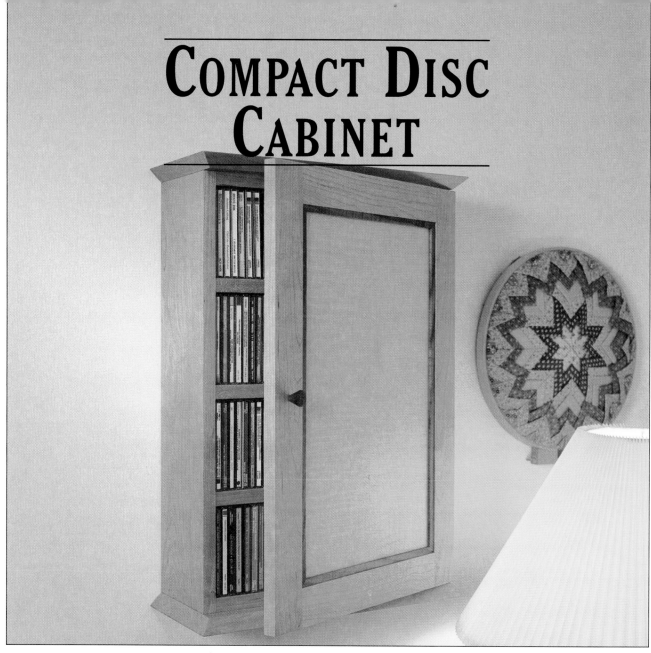

The solid-cherry cabinet and door frame highlight the curly-maple door panel in this compact disc cabinet.

It didn't take long for the compact disc to replace the LP and cassette tape as *the* format for recorded music. For most of us, that means coming up with new storage systems to keep our growing collections organized. Sure, you can buy all manner of CD cabinets, shelves, and racks. Or you can make your own storage cabinet instead—and do some beautiful woodworking at the same time.

This cabinet will hold 150 CDs, plenty of room for the collection of an avid music lover. But the size of the cabinet can be adjusted to fit your own CD collection. It was designed to be equally at home hanging on a wall, or standing on a table or floor cabinet. The construction is simple—rabbet and dado joints for the case, and mortise-and-tenon joints for the door. The back fits into a rabbet that is cut into the sides, top, and bottom. The walnut trim was glued to the door panel after assembly. The panel is a ¼-inch piece of plywood that is veneered on both sides with curly maple. It's small enough that you can veneer it yourself with the instructions provided. Or you can use a piece of stock plywood.

The cabinet was finished with a homemade wipe-on oil-varnish mixture, which deepened the color of both the maple and the cherry but enhanced the contrast between the two woods. Since the cabinet doesn't have to stand up to rigorous use like a table or chair, it only needed two coats. (See "Oil/Varnish-Blend Finishes" on page 22.)

FRONT VIEW

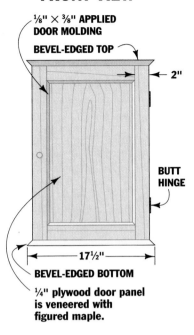

⅛" × ⅜" APPLIED DOOR MOLDING

BEVEL-EDGED TOP

2"

BUTT HINGE

17½"

BEVEL-EDGED BOTTOM

¼" plywood door panel is veneered with figured maple.

SIDE VIEW

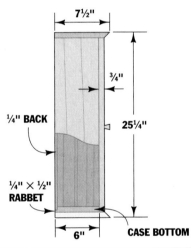

7½"

¾"

¼" BACK

25¼"

¼" × ½" RABBET

6"

CASE BOTTOM

EXPLODED VIEW

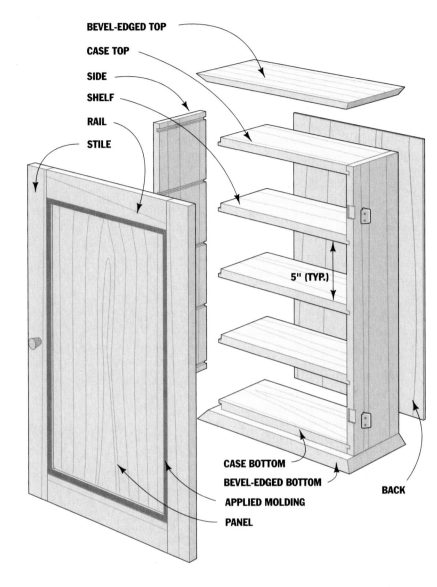

BEVEL-EDGED TOP

CASE TOP

SIDE

SHELF

RAIL

STILE

5" (TYP.)

CASE BOTTOM

BEVEL-EDGED BOTTOM

APPLIED MOLDING

PANEL

BACK

MATERIALS LIST

PART	QTY.	DIMENSIONS
Sides	2	¾" × 6" × 23¾"
Top and bottom	2	¾" × 6" × 15"
Bevel-edged top and bottom	2	¾" × 7½" × 17½"
Shelves	3	¾" × 5¾" × 15"
Stiles	2	¾" × 2" × 23¾"
Rails	2	¾" × 2" × 15"
Turned knob	1	¾" × ¾" × ¾"
Applied door molding*	2	⅛" × ⅜" × 19¾"
	2	⅛" × ⅜" × 12"

PART	QTY.	DIMENSIONS
Door panel	1	+/- 5/16" × 12¾" × 20½"
Back	1	¼" × 15½" × 23¼"

HARDWARE

Butt hinges (2)

Bullet catch (optional) (1)

#6 × ¾" flathead wood screws (12)

*Miter to length after door is assembled.

Procedure

1 **Cut the parts to the sizes provided in the Materials List.**

2 **Cut the dadoes in the sides.** It's crucial that each shelf have 5 inches of vertical space to accommodate the CDs. (CDs measure 4⅞ inches high, and the extra ⅛ inch will accommodate boxed sets of CDs.) Lay out the shelf locations on both sides, then mark where the dadoes will be cut for each shelf. Cut the dadoes with a dado blade set for about ¼-inch-wide cut. The exact width of the dado is not crucial, but maintain the 5-inch spacing between the shelves. Run the sides across the blade, locating the cuts with the rip fence. Cut the dadoes for the case top and bottom first, with the same fence setting. Then refer to *Front View* on page 101 to reset the fence for each of the other shelves. Because the tongues on the shelves are not centered, the placement of each pair of dadoes requires its own setup.

3 **Cut the rabbets.** Set up a dado cutter on your table saw to make a cut at least ½ inch wide. Attach a wooden auxiliary fence at least 1 inch thick to the saw fence. Position the auxiliary fence over the blade. Raise the blade into the auxiliary fence to cut an arc for clearance, and set the blade height at ½ inch. Then set the fence so ¼ inch of the blade is exposed. Cut a rabbet on a test piece and adjust the fence and blade height so the tongue fits perfectly in the dadoes. Then rabbet all the parts. Cut the rabbets for the back in the sides, top, and bottom with the same setup.

4 **Assemble the case.** Clamp and glue the case top, bottom, and shelves to the case sides. Before the glue dries, set the back into the rabbets to square the case. Fasten the back to the case with #6 × ¾-inch flathead wood screws. Predrill for the screws through the back and into the solid wood.

5 **Make the bevel-edged top and bottom.** Make the 45-degree cuts on the front and ends of the bevel-edged top and bottom on the table saw. Check the second end miter cut, which determines the length of these parts, against the cabinet. Round-over the sharp corners with a block plane, then clean up the bevel cuts with a block plane and sandpaper. Also, slightly round-over the top and bottom edges of the sides. Clamp and glue the outside top and bottom to the case top and bottom so the base of the miters meets the edges of the case parts. Be stingy with glue here, and let it tack up a bit before tightening the clamps. Otherwise, the parts will slide around.

6 **Make the door panel.** You need to make the door panel before the frame so that you can accurately size the groove that it fits into in the frame. You can use standard ¼-inch hardwood plywood and just cut the panel to size. Or you can give the panel a more personal touch by veneering it with a nicer-looking wood, as shown in *Veneering Your Own Panels* on page 104.

7 **Make the door frame.** *Door Details*, below, shows the proportions of the mortise-and-tenon joints. Using a haunched tenon adds some strength to the joint, plus you don't have to stop the groove in the stiles. Rout the mortises first, as shown in "Cutting Mortise-and-Tenon Joints" on page 98. Cut the groove in the rails and stiles on the table saw, making two passes with a rip blade. Then cut the tenons to fit the mortises. Cut the haunch on the tenons with a back saw.

DOOR DETAILS

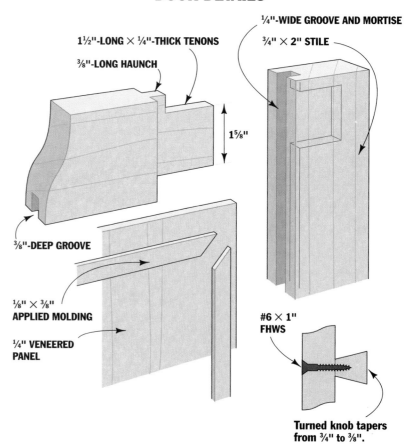

1½"-LONG × ¼"-THICK TENONS

⅜"-LONG HAUNCH

¼"-WIDE GROOVE AND MORTISE

¾" × 2" STILE

1⅝"

⅜"-DEEP GROOVE

⅛" × ⅜" APPLIED MOLDING

¼" VENEERED PANEL

#6 × 1" FHWS

Turned knob tapers from ¾" to ⅜".

8 **Assemble the door frame.** Glue the frame joints together, being sure to slide the panel in place as you go. Clamp the joints tight, and check that the assembly is flat with a straightedge.

9 **Cut and apply the door molding.** Miter the door molding to fit around the inside of the frame. Cut the long pieces and spring them into place, then cut the short ones. Apply a very thin line of yellow glue around the perimeter of the panel and set the molding in place. Use spring clamps to hold the molding down, as shown in **Photo 1**.

10 **Hang the door.** Trim the edges of the door so there is a $\frac{1}{16}$-inch gap at the top and bottom. The sides of the door should be flush with the sides of the cabinet. Cut the mortises for the butt hinges in the doors, then mount the hinges. Set the door in place with a $\frac{1}{16}$-inch shim under the bottom edge. Cut marks with a utility knife into the inside edge of the side to locate the mortises. Cut the mortises and attach the hinges to the side, but insert just one screw in each hinge and test the fit. That way, if you have to move the hinge slightly you can use the other hinge holes.

Attach a knob to the door. The simple turned cove worked nicely, but you could buy or make a different one to give it your own personal touch. Install a bullet catch in the bevel-edged case bottom to keep the door closed.

11 **Finish the project.** Sand the cabinet and door. Wipe the oil-varnish blend onto the parts liberally with a clean rag, as shown in **Photos 2** and **3**. Keep the finish wet for a few minutes, then wipe all the remaining finish off with dry rags. If the finish gets too tacky, loosen it up by wiping on more finish. Be sure all the parts are dry when you're done. Two coats are sufficient.

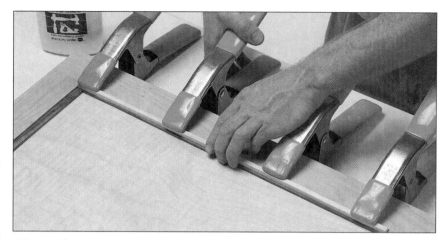

Photo 1: **Large spring clamps pull the molding into the corner of the frame. Strips of $\frac{1}{4} \times \frac{1}{4}$-inch scrap wood make the job easier.**

Photo 2: **Lay the parts out horizontally. A pair of 2 $\times$ 2 beams set on saw horses makes a good stage. Wipe on the finish and wet all the surfaces thoroughly.**

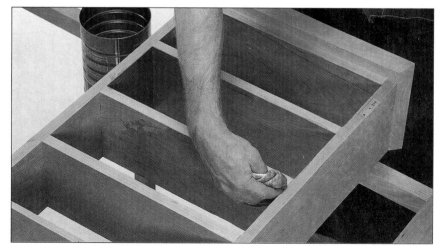

Photo 3: **Wipe the finish off the case, working from the inside to the outside. If it's too tacky, just wet it again with finish.**

SHOP SOLUTIONS: Veneering Your Own Panels

MAKING VENEER SEAMS

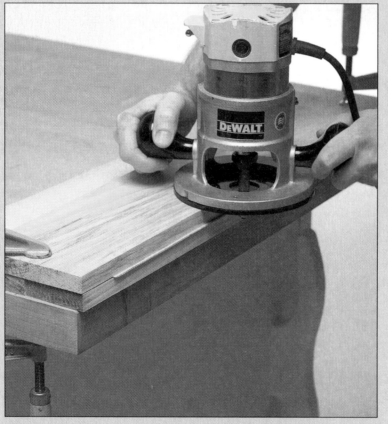

¾" PLYWOOD OR SOLID WOOD

Flush-trim both veneers to a perfectly straight edge.

Two pieces of veneer face-to-face

Make this edge dead straight.

Photo 1: Clamp the two pieces of veneer between two pieces of plywood with ¹⁄₁₆ inch extending beyond the edge. To prevent the veneer from chipping out, make a climb cut, working *with* the direction the router rotates.

Making your own veneered panels lets you choose from a much broader range of wood species than if you limit your choice to solid stock, or standard hardwood plywood. All sorts of figured and exotic woods are available in veneer form, and most suppliers will provide small amounts, like the eight square feet needed for the panel in the Compact Disc Cabinet's door.

You can apply veneer to any kind of panel—plywood, particleboard, etc., but you must veneer both sides of the panel to maintain structural balance. If you veneer just one side, the panel will invariably bow or twist from the imbalance.

If you're making a relatively narrow panel, you may be able to get a piece of veneer wide enough to cover the entire piece. That way you won't have to deal with seams.

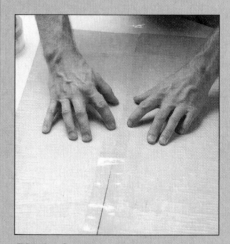

Photo 2: Lay the seams together on a flat surface, butt the edges tightly together and apply a strip of plastic packaging tape along the entire seam. Unlike paper veneer tapes, the plastic tape peels off cleanly and easily after the glue has cured.

But for wider panels, you'll have to make some edge seams. Seams can also be used intentionally to create bookmatch, diamond, and other patterns with the veneer.

If you need to make a seam, you can tape the two pieces together face-to-face and run them over the jointer to get a perfect joint. A more reliable approach, especially for figured veneers, is to clamp the two veneers face-to-face between two pieces of plywood, one of which has a perfectly straight edge, and flush-trim them to the straight edge, as shown in *Making Veneer Seams* and in **Photo 1** on the opposite page. Then tape the pieces together using veneer tape or clear plastic packaging tape, as shown in **Photo 2**.

To make the door panel for the Compact Disc Cabinet, start with a piece of ¼-inch plywood that's about 1 inch oversize in both length and width. If possible, orient the grain on the plywood so it runs in the short direction across the panel. This continues the alternating orientation of the plies that

Photo 3: Clamp all the press bars on lightly. Tighten the center ones first, then tighten the ones on the sides.

make up the panel. Cut the veneer for the front and back to the same size as the panel.

You can glue veneer to a panel with standard yellow glue. The goal during gluing is twofold: get the glue-up under clamps before the glue starts to tack, and apply even pressure to the entire surface while keeping the panel flat. To achieve the first objective, spread the glue with a small paint roller

or notched trowel. Apply glue to the panel only, and lay the panel onto the veneer. If you apply glue to the veneer it will quickly start to curl and it's likely to crack as you try to flatten it out. To get even clamping pressure, make a veneer press, as shown below in *Simple Veneer Press*.

The veneer press is composed of two plywood or particleboard cauls cut to the same size as the veneer and panel. The cauls help distribute the clamping pressure across the whole panel. Additionally, use a set of press bars to convey the clamp pressure onto the center portion of the panel. The press bars are lengths of solid wood with a slight crown along the length of one edge. The crown forces the cauls to apply pressure from the center out to the edges so you only need two clamps for each pair of bars, one clamp at either end. Form the crown on the jointer with a hand plane, disc sander, or belt sander. **Photo 3** shows the completed glue-up. After the glue has cured, remove the panel and cut it to finished size.

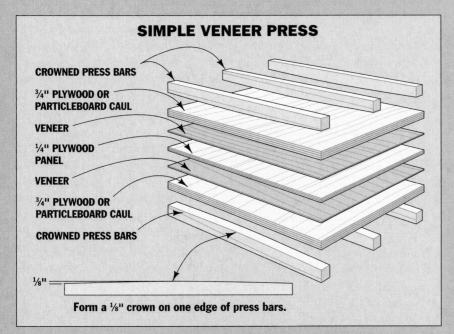

SIMPLE VENEER PRESS

CROWNED PRESS BARS
¾" PLYWOOD OR PARTICLEBOARD CAUL
VENEER
¼" PLYWOOD PANEL
VENEER
¾" PLYWOOD OR PARTICLEBOARD CAUL
CROWNED PRESS BARS

⅛"

Form a ⅛" crown on one edge of press bars.

KITCHEN CART

This oak cart with a maple butcher-block top will extend your counter space or work as a mobile island for preparing and serving food.

If there's never enough counter space in your kitchen, this rolling cart will help solve the problem. Use the top of the cart for food preparation, or to hold a microwave or toaster oven. The two lower shelves will hold lesser used appliances or large pots and pans that don't fit in a drawer. And you can easily move the cart right where you need it.

The base of this cart is made of oak that was colored with a walnut oil stain, though you might want to stain it to match your own kitchen cabinetry. The top of the cart, a chunk of maple "butcher block," is

made by cutting plain-sawn stock into strips and gluing the strips together on edge. This gives you the classic butcher-block look—a surface of predominantly quarter-sawn, or edge grain, strips. The nice thing about gluing up stock like this is that it allows you to make a thick, robust surface from commonly available 4/4 stock.

Since the cart is apt to see heavy use, it is finished with a durable polyurethane varnish that will stand up to the rigors of KP duty. If you intend to use the top as a cutting board, you may want to finish it with an oil or oil/varnish

blend. While these finishes don't offer the protection that polyurethane does, they are much easier to renew periodically. If, on the other hand, you want to keep the maple top from yellowing, consider a water based urethane.

You could also use the cart outdoors on a deck or patio. If that's your plan, consider using a wood that holds up better against the weather, like cedar, redwood, or white oak, and a more durable finish like spar varnish. You'll also want to use larger casters or wheels so the cart will move more easily over bumpier outdoor surfaces.

Procedure

1 Cut the parts to the sizes given in the Materials List.

2 Cut the mortises and tenons. Lay out the mortises on two adjacent faces of each leg, as shown in *Mortise-and-Tenon Details.* The mortises are centered in the thickness of the leg, and all four legs are identical. Refer to pages 98–99 for detailed instructions and for jigs for making accurate mortise-and-tenon joints. Chop the ends of the routed mortises square with a ⅜-inch chisel. Drill the holes for the towel bars after cutting all the mortises. You can put a towel bar on one end of the cart or both. Profile the edges of the legs with a ¼-inch roundover bit. Note that the tenon shoulders on the top rails are ⅜ inch but only ¼ inch on the shelf rails, as shown in *Mortise-and-Tenon Details.*

3 Miter the tenons. Centering the mortises in the legs limits their depth. Mitering the tenons on the rails is the best way to use the limited mortise depth to fullest advantage. Cut the miters on the table saw, as shown in **Photo 1**. Set the blade high enough to just complete the miter cut. Then clamp a stop to the rip fence that will position each tenon in relation to the angled blade. When you make the cut, the waste piece will be free to drop away from the blade.

4 Assemble the base. First, glue and clamp the side rails and towel bar to the legs, and check that the assemblies are square and flat. Then glue the front and back rails to the side assemblies. Miter the ends of the corner blocks and screw them into the top rails with #6 × 1¼-inch flathead wood screws.

MORTISE-AND-TENON DETAILS

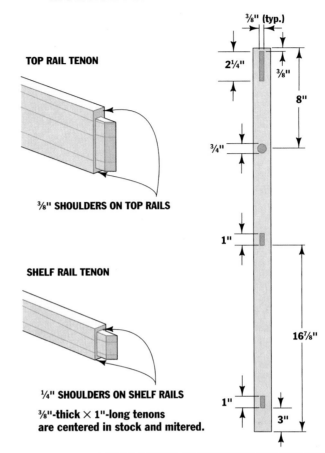

TOP RAIL TENON

⅜" SHOULDERS ON TOP RAILS

SHELF RAIL TENON

¼" SHOULDERS ON SHELF RAILS
⅜"-thick × 1"-long tenons are centered in stock and mitered.

Photo 1: **Miter the tenons using a stop block clamped to the fence so the waste piece can fall free.**

EXPLODED VIEW

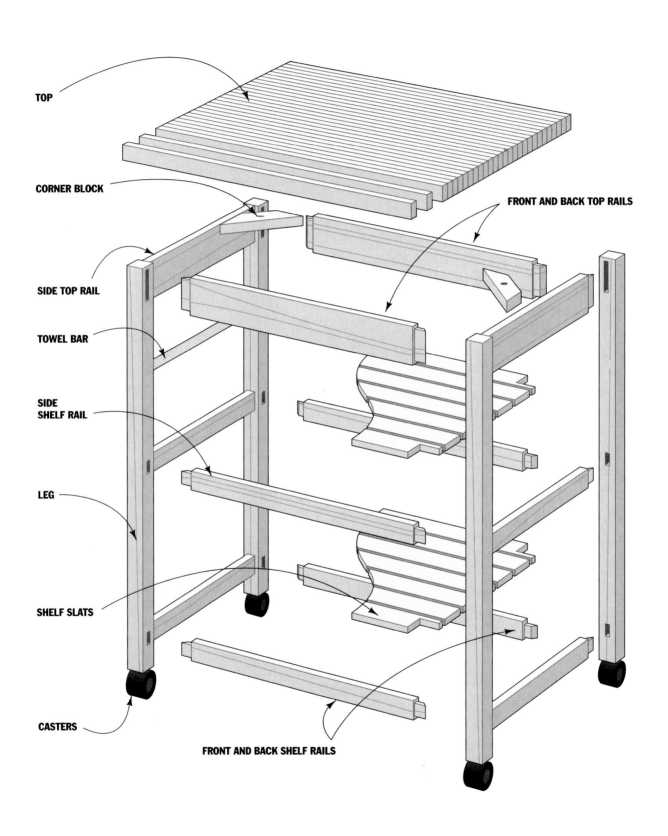

TOP

CORNER BLOCK

FRONT AND BACK TOP RAILS

SIDE TOP RAIL

TOWEL BAR

SIDE
SHELF RAIL

LEG

SHELF SLATS

CASTERS

FRONT AND BACK SHELF RAILS

TOP VIEW (THROUGH RAILS)

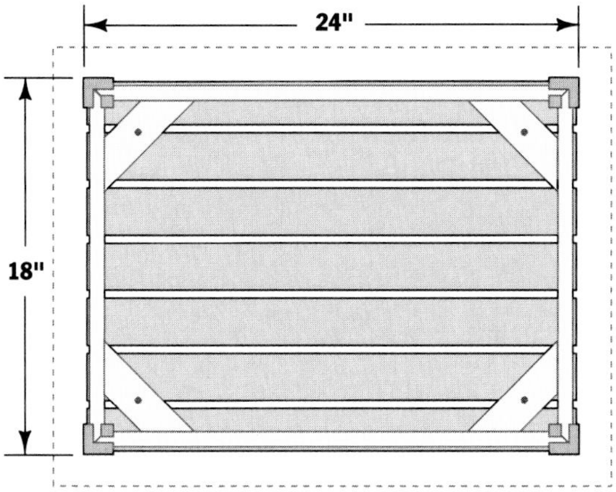
24"
18"

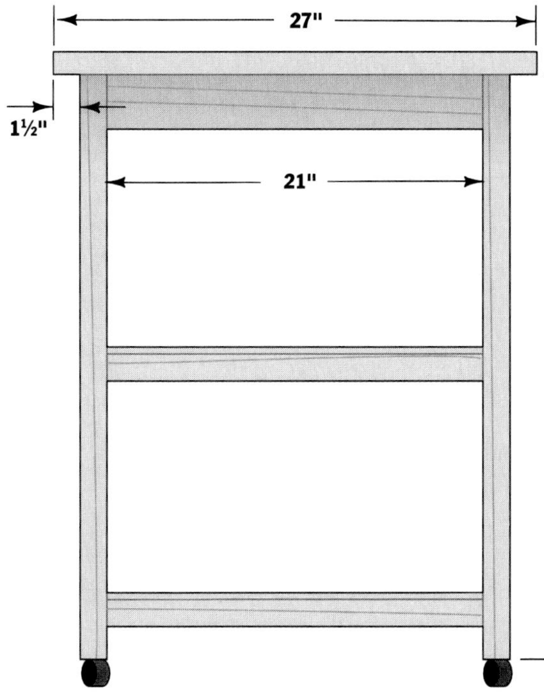
27"
1½"
21"
32¼"

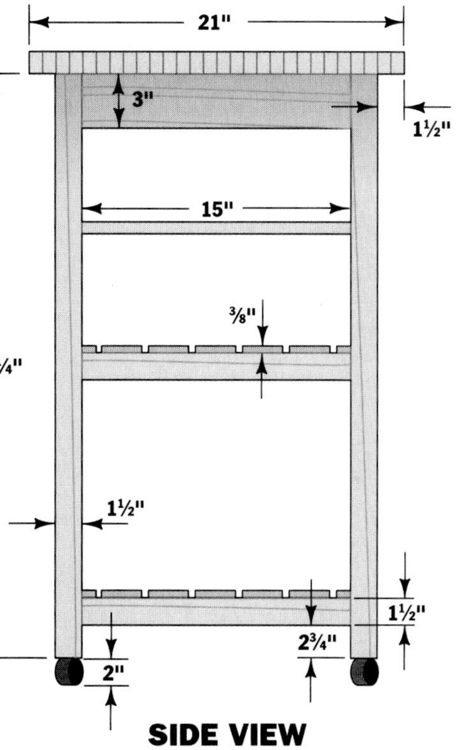
21"
3"
1½"
15"
⅜"
1½"
1½"
2¾"
2"

FRONT VIEW **SIDE VIEW**

MATERIALS LIST

PARTS	QTY.	DIMENSIONS
Legs	4	1½" × 1½" × 32¼"
Top rails	2	¾" × 3" × 17"
Side, front, and back top rails	2	¾" × 3" × 23"
Shelf rails	4	¾" × 1½" × 17"
Side, front, and back shelf rails	4	¾" × 1½" × 23"
Towel bar	1	¾" × 17"
*Shelf slats	14	⅜" × 2¼" × 23⅜"
Top	1	1¼" × 21" × 27"
Corner blocks	4	¾" × 2" × 6"

HARDWARE

2" casters (4)
#8 × 1¼" roundhead wood screws (4)
#6 × 1" flathead wood screws (60)
#6 × 1¼" flathead wood screws (8)
#8 flat washers (4)

*Resaw the slats from 4/4 stock and leave them as thick as possible.

5 **Shape the shelf slats.** Cut notches in the corners of the front and back slats so they fit around the legs, as shown in *Shelf Slat Detail.* Profile all the top edges of the slats, including the notched corners, with a small roundover or chamfer bit. Predrill two ⅛-inch holes at either end of each slat, locating the holes ⁹⁄₁₆ inch in from the end and edge of each slat. Countersink the holes for #6 × 1-inch flathead wood screws. Sand all the slats to 180 grit. Attach them after finishing.

6 **Make the butcher-block top.** Plane all the stock for the top to a uniform thickness. Rip as many 1¼-inch-wide strips as needed to get the full width of the top, as shown in *Making a Butcher-Block Top.* If your stock is ¾ inch thick, you'll need 28 strips, but you can leave the stock thicker and use fewer strips.

It is best to glue up the top in two sections. Putting the strips together will require spreading glue on a lot of surfaces and you don't want the glue to start setting up before you're ready. Gluing one half at a time also means you have fewer pieces to try to keep aligned. Clamp the strips together on a flat surface with a layer of wax paper underneath to catch the excess glue. Another advantage of this approach is that you can run each half of the top through a small planer to true up the top and bottom surfaces. (Scrape off the excess glue first to keep from dulling the knives.) After you've planed the halves, glue them together. Add a stopped spline or a few biscuits to this center joint to make the halves perfectly flush. Profile the top edges of the top with a ¼-inch roundover bit.

SHELF SLAT DETAIL

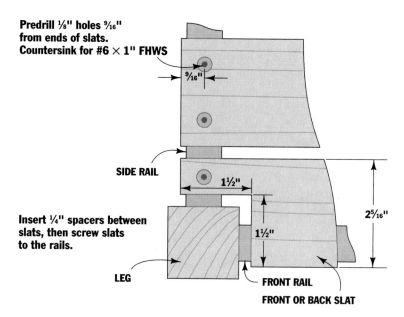

Predrill ⅛" holes ⁹⁄₁₆" from ends of slats. Countersink for #6 × 1" FHWS

⁹⁄₁₆"

SIDE RAIL

1½"

Insert ¼" spacers between slats, then screw slats to the rails.

LEG

1½"

2⁵⁄₁₆"

FRONT RAIL

FRONT OR BACK SLAT

Cut 1½" × 1½" notches in corners of front and back slats.

MAKING A BUTCHER-BLOCK TOP

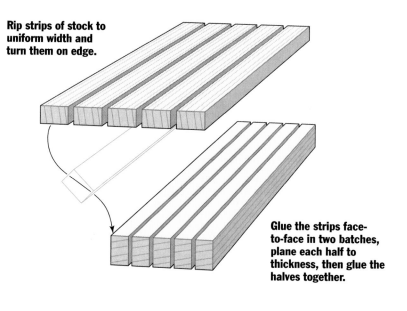

Rip strips of stock to uniform width and turn them on edge.

Glue the strips face-to-face in two batches, plane each half to thickness, then glue the halves together.

Add stopped spline or biscuits to align center joint.

7 **Finish the cart.** Apply an oil-based dye stain liberally with a rag to the base and shelf slats, as shown in **Photo 2**. After a few minutes, rub all the excess stain off, as shown in **Photo 3.** Repeat the process to darken the wood more. Allow at least two days to cure, then brush on polyurethane varnish to both the base and the top, as shown in **Photo 4.**

8 **Attach the shelf slats.** Lay all the slats in place across the bottom rails. They should extend beyond the rails ³⁄₁₆ inch on each end. Cut a dozen spacers from ¼-inch plywood, Masonite, or solid wood, and insert them between the slats. Hold a straightedge against the ends of the slats to align them. Predrill into the rails and screw the slats home with #6 × 1-inch flathead wood screws. Repeat the process to complete the second shelf.

9 **Attach the top.** Drill ¼-inch holes in the center of the corner blocks. Center the top on the base. Predrill ⅛-inch holes up through the corner blocks into the top. Insert #8 × 1¼ flathead wood screws with flat washers through the corner blocks. The large holes in the corner blocks allow the top to expand and contract slightly.

10 **Attach the casters.** Use casters designated for hard floors, and choose the stem-and-socket type that's mounted in a single hole drilled in the center of the legs. The plate-mount version requires that you drill holes too close to the edges of the legs.

Photo 2: Wipe on the oil stain liberally to the base and shelf slats. Give it a few minutes to soak into the wood.

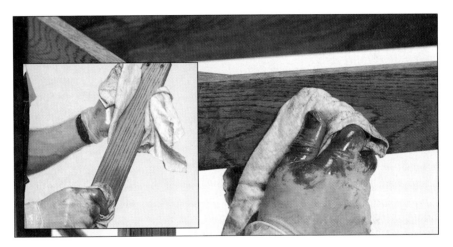

Photo 3: Wipe off the excess stain with a clean cloth. Then wipe all the surfaces dry to be sure you got it all off. To avoid leaving fingerprints on the slats, hold a rag in each hand while wiping off the stain.

Photo 4: Brush on clear satin polyurethane to all the parts. Be sure to finish both sides of the top and the shelf slats. Apply at least two coats, sanding lightly with 320-grit paper between coats.

GAME BOX

You'll get hours of pleasure from this game board, which slides out to reveal a storage box for all your chess and checker pieces. Creating the checkerboard will be a pleasure, too. The pattern is created by spraying colored lacquer onto a standard piece of birch plywood. The trick is in the masking.

Checkers and chess are time-less games of skill and strategy. Unfortunately, the folding cardboard game boards you can buy for a buck last only a short time before falling apart like an old paperback book. This board will last a lifetime, and will give you a place to keep your checkers and chess pieces from getting lost.

Many plans for game boards involve complicated woodworking techniques, like inlaying or assembling veneers or doweling together individual blocks of contrasting woods. Using some of the finishing techniques presented in this book, you can make a game board with far less effort in just a few hours.

The game board itself is made from a piece of standard ½-inch-

thick birch plywood. The dark squares are sprayed with colored lacquer; the light ones are left natural with a clear finish. The game board slides in grooves in the solid cherry sides of the box. The corners of the box are mitered and reinforced with walnut feather keys after assembly. The handle makes for easy transport so you can play in style anywhere.

EXPLODED VIEW

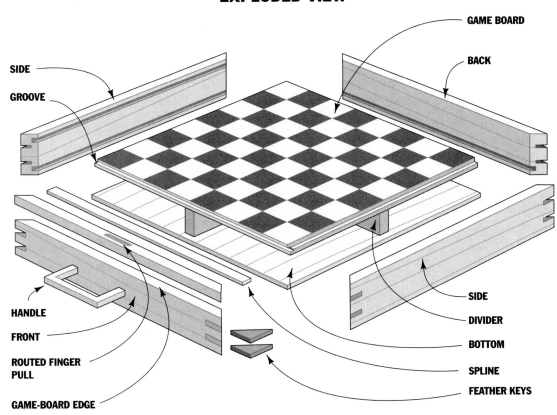

SIDE

GROOVE

GAME BOARD

BACK

HANDLE

FRONT

ROUTED FINGER PULL

GAME-BOARD EDGE

SIDE

DIVIDER

BOTTOM

SPLINE

FEATHER KEYS

MATERIALS LIST

PART	QTY.	DIMENSIONS
Sides and back	3	$\frac{3}{4}" \times 2\frac{1}{2}" \times 17\frac{1}{2}"$
Front*	1	$\frac{3}{4}" \times 2" \times 17\frac{1}{2}"$
Game-board edge†	1	$\frac{1}{2}" \times \frac{3}{4}" \times 17\frac{1}{2}"$
Game board (birch plywood)	1	$\frac{1}{2}" \times 16" \times 16\frac{1}{2}"$
Dividers	2	$\frac{3}{4}" \times 1\frac{1}{2}" \times 16"$
Bottom (plywood)	1	$\frac{1}{4}" \times 16\frac{1}{2}" \times 16\frac{1}{2}"$
Feather keys‡	8	$\frac{1}{8}" \times 1\frac{1}{8}" \times 2\frac{1}{4}"$
Handle	1	

*Make $2\frac{3}{4}"$ wide to start

†Rip from front before assembling box.

‡Plane to fit after cutting kerfs.

FRONT VIEW

DIVIDER

$2\frac{1}{2}"$

$\frac{1}{2}"$-veneered-plywood top slides in grooves to access storage box.

TOP VIEW

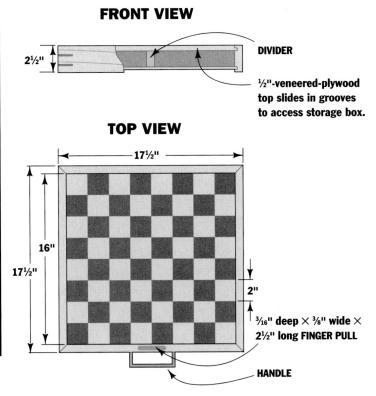

$17\frac{1}{2}"$

16"

$17\frac{1}{2}"$

2"

$\frac{3}{16}"$ deep $\times$ $\frac{3}{8}"$ wide $\times$ $2\frac{1}{2}"$ long FINGER PULL

HANDLE

Procedure

1 Make the game board. Cut the game board to the size listed in the Materials List. Rabbet the two side edges to form the ¼ × ¼-inch tongues. Cut the rabbets with a dado blade buried in an auxiliary wood fence, or a straight bit in the router table. Cutting the tongue leaves you with a 16-inch square game board surface. Sand both sides of the top and round all the edges slightly.

2 Create the game-board grid. The dark squares of the game-board are colored with a walnut spray lacquer, also called toner, that's available in spray cans. The challenge is carefully masking off the light, unstained squares. First, apply a sealer coat of lacquer sanding sealer, or a thin coat of clear wiping varnish. You could even use regular lacquer for the sealer, since that is used for the top coat as well. If you use the wiping varnish, be sure to allow three or four days for the finish to dry before applying the lacquer top coat.

Once the sealer is dry, cover the top with strips of clear plastic packaging tape, as shown in **Photo 1**. You want the tape to be perfectly flat, with no wrinkles or bubbles. Wrinkles in the tape will act like little straws, pulling the toner onto the masked-off blocks. Mark off the 2-inch hash marks along each edge of the board with a felt-tip pen that will show on the clear tape. With a straightedge and sharp utility knife, cut along the lines. You want to cut deeply enough to slice through the tape and the veneer, as shown in **Photo 2**. Cutting through the veneer forms a tiny moat around each square that keeps the spray stain from bleeding onto the unstained squares. Peel the tape off the squares to be stained, as shown in **Photo 3**. Press down the remaining squares of tape, using a rubber stamp

roller, wooden veneer wheel, or a small block of softwood with rounded edges. Spray the exposed squares with a dark lacquer toner, as shown in **Photo 4** on the opposite page. Apply *very* light coats because a heavy, wet coat is more likely to bleed under the tape onto the masked-off squares. Follow the recommended drying time between coats, but don't sand in between coats or you'll cut through the toner.

Once the stain is dark enough and the last coat is dry, peel off the remaining tape; see **Photo 5** on the opposite page. If any of the toner has bled onto the masked-off squares, remove it using a Q-Tip moistened with lacquer thinner. If necessary, scrape it off with a single-edge razor. Don't worry about removing the sealer coat because the clear top coat will re-cover any bare spots.

Photo 1: Lay down strips of packaging tape, overlapping the strips about ¼ inch and wrapping the tape over the edges of the game board. Use a rubber roller or wooden veneer wheel to press down the tape.

Photo 2: Mark off the 2-inch squares along all four edges of the board. Slice through the tape and the veneer.

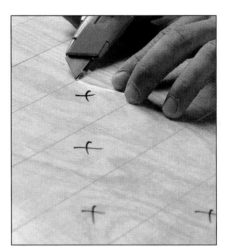

Photo 3: Use your fingernails or the tip of a razor to lift the corner of the tape from every other square.

Photo 4: Spray the board with three or four very light coats of a dark-colored lacquer toner.

FRONT DETAIL

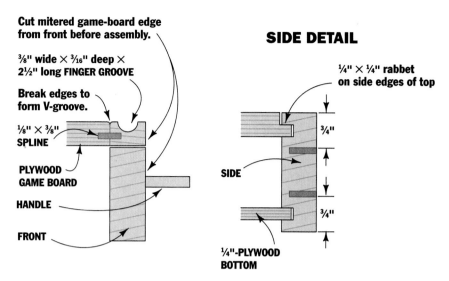

Cut mitered game-board edge from front before assembly.

⅜" wide × 3/16" deep × 2½" long FINGER GROOVE

Break edges to form V-groove.

⅛" × ⅜" SPLINE

PLYWOOD GAME BOARD

HANDLE

FRONT

SIDE DETAIL

¼" × ¼" rabbet on side edges of top

¾"

SIDE

¾"

¼"-PLYWOOD BOTTOM

Photo 5: **Lift the tape carefully. Remove any toner from the unstained squares, and spray the game board with a coat of clear lacquer.**

CLAMPING A MITERED BOX

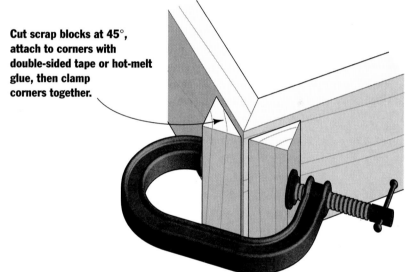

Cut scrap blocks at 45°, attach to corners with double-sided tape or hot-melt glue, then clamp corners together.

3 Cut and groove the box parts. Plane the front, back, and sides of the box; rip them to width, but leave them a few inches long for now. The front of the box is ¼ inch wider than the back and sides. This is because the top edge of the front gets ripped off and attached to the plywood game board; the extra width allows for the saw kerf. For now, treat the front just like the sides and back. Cut a groove along the bottom edge of the sides, front, and back, for the bottom, as shown in *Side Detail*. Because the plywood is not likely to be a true ¼ inch thick, make two passes with a saw blade, and use the plywood bottom itself to gauge the fit. Also, cut a groove along the top edge of the sides (but not the front or the back) for the top to ride in. Use the tongue on the top to locate and size the groove, so the top will be flush with or a hair under the top edges of the sides.

4 Cut the joints and assemble the box. Miter the ends of the box parts using the game-board top as a guide for length. Rip the front to width—it should equal the width of the sides less the thickness of the top. Mark the offcut from the front, so when it is attached to the game-board top it will match the grain on the front. Sand the bottom and inside faces of the box parts.

The mitered ends of the box parts won't form a very strong glue joint, but "sizing" the miters will improve the bond. To size the miters, apply a thin coat of glue and let it absorb into the surface of the miters for a couple of minutes or until it tacks over. Then apply a fresh coat of glue and assemble the box. Apply glue to the grooves for the bottom. Attach angled corner blocks to the sides with hot-melt glue or double-sided tape and clamp the box together with C-clamps, as shown in *Clamping a Mitered Box*.

5 Add feather keys to the miter joints. After the glue dries, clean up the outside corners of the box. Make a jig like the one shown in *Splined Miter Jig* to cradle the box. Then cut two saw kerfs into each corner on the table saw, as shown in **Photo 6**, below. (You'll need to tape the mitered game-board edge back onto the front of the box so the box can be clamped evenly into the jig.) The saw kerfs should be ¾ inch in from the top and bottom edges of the box, as shown in *Side Detail* on page 115. Cut walnut splines and glue them into the kerfs. Trim the splines on the band saw and sand them flush to the sides, while sanding the outside of the whole box.

6 Rout the finger pull. Cut the mitered piece you ripped from the front to match the thickness of the top exactly. Lay out the ends of the finger pull onto both faces. Chuck a ⅜-inch-diameter core-box bit in a router and set it for a ³⁄₁₆-inch-deep cut. Rout the finger-pull groove in the center of the mitered edge. Because the piece is so small, this step is easiest to do on a router table. If you don't have a router table, rout the groove after gluing the edge to the top. In that case, guide the router with either an edge guide or a straightedge clamped to the top.

7 Attach the mitered edge of the front to the top. Cut a ⅛-inch-deep saw kerf in both the game-board top and the mitered edge, as shown in *Front Detail* on page 115. Make a spline to fit the grooves and glue it into the top. Trim the ends of the spline so they follow the tongue on the edges of the top.

Break the edges of both the top and the mitered edge so there's a small V-groove at the joint—you don't want to sand this joint flush because that would foul up the stained

SPLINED MITER JIG

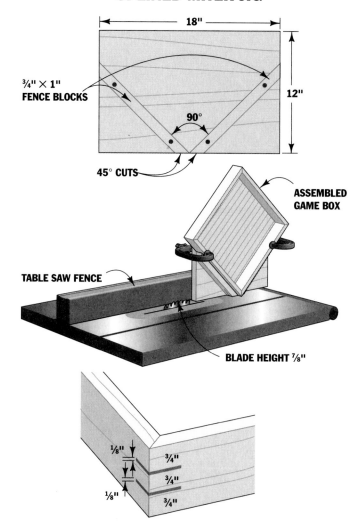

18"

12"

¾" × 1" FENCE BLOCKS

90°

45° CUTS

ASSEMBLED GAME BOX

TABLE SAW FENCE

BLADE HEIGHT ⅞"

⅛" ¾"

¾"

⅛" ¾"

Photo 6: **Set the blade height to ⅞ inch. Clamp the box into the jig, set the fence, and make the cuts with the jig riding snugly against the fence.**

squares. Glue the mitered edge onto the top, and clean off any excess glue right away. If you have a biscuit joiner, you can use a few biscuits here instead of a spline, but be sure to keep the biscuits clear of where the finger pull will be routed.

8 Make the dividers. The box has two half-lapped dividers that break the interior of the box into four compartments. Cut the dividers to size. Mark the notch at the center of one of the dividers, as shown in *Divider Detail.* Cut the notches on the table saw with a standard cross-cut blade, using the miter gauge to guide the dividers across the blade. Set the fence so the blade cuts inside either one of the notch layout lines. Now you can make both outside cuts with the fence in the same setting. Remove the waste in between the end cuts without using the fence.

You can divide the interior of the box into smaller compartments by adding more half-lapped dividers along one of the center dividers. Glue and clamp the dividers together, checking that they are square to each other. The assembled dividers can be press-fit into the box, or you can screw through the bottom to anchor them permanently.

9 Finish the box. Sand the box, then lay out the pieces to finish, as shown in **Photo 7.** Apply three or four light coats of clear lacquer.

Now that the game-board top has a buildup of clear finish on it, you can lightly sand the surface with 600-grit wet/dry sandpaper to knock down the ridges raised by the razor cuts. Give the top a final coat of spray lacquer. Apply wax to the tongue to smooth the sliding action of the top.

10 Attach a handle of your choice. You can make a wooden han-

DIVIDER DETAIL

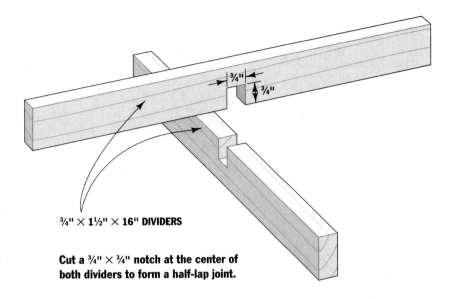

¾" × ¾"

¾" × 1½" × 16" DIVIDERS

Cut a ¾" × ¾" notch at the center of both dividers to form a half-lap joint.

Photo 7: **Remove the dividers and top, and support all the parts with tabs of scrap wood so the edges are raised. Apply three or four light coats of lacquer in thin, even coats.**

dle for the game board to make it easier to carry, but be sure it is well anchored to the front of the box with screws or dowels. A simpler solution is to buy a handle that gets bolted through the front of the box, like the one shown in the photo on page 112.

INDEX